BLIND
IN ONE EYE

A STORY ABOUT SEEING THE POSSIBILITIES

DAVID R. FORD

Printed in the United States of America.

Library of Congress Control Number: 2010935495

CREDITS:

Cover and Layout Design: Hank Isaac, hank@riverrockcreative.com

Cover Photograph: Elizabeth and David Ford

FOREWORD

While this is a true story, it is only *my* version of events that took control of my life. The others intimately involved in the story—my wife, my loving (and beloved) adoptive parents, the "Keepers" and "Throwaways," my birth parents—would all have had different stories to tell, if they had chosen to do so. I hope that they forgive my failings in telling the story and find some value in seeing it through my eyes. I have changed their names in this book for their benefit, not mine; I am grateful to have been inextricably drawn into their lives.

I dedicate this book to Tibby, for her love, constancy and blind devotion mixed with great expectations—not to mention her willingness to re-read, and critique passionately, the many drafts of this story that I've dropped on her. (I only wish that she liked the title as much as I do.)

1

Thirty years was a long time to wonder if I would ever meet my brother. But finding him would feel like a side trip by the time the search had led me to its real destination. The most remarkable discoveries seem to come while looking for something else, as long as you're open to the possibilities.

Greg would turn out not to match the image my wife Tibby and I had in our minds. We didn't know that at the time, so there was hopeful excitement in Tibby's voice when she called me from her office. It pulled my attention to her words, drawing me away from the pile of papers on my desk.

"Motty asked me if you had an older brother." Tibby was trying, unsuccessfully, to mute the effect of her news on me; she was the calm one in our relationship. "She said she sat across the aisle on the subway from a guy who looked just like you, same build, everything, just older." Motty was my wife's friend and co-worker; she had seen me often enough to picture someone as my brother, but would not have had the confidence to approach the guy and ask him the question.

"What did you tell her?" It shouldn't have been a hard question for anyone else to answer: Does he or doesn't he have a brother? Few people knew that I was adopted; even fewer knew that I had a mystery brother.

I suppose *this* would have been the moment, if I had that magical power to go back and change events, that stands out as the time and place to revisit, the moment where my new life was beginning. If I had been the only factor in the equation, I don't think I would choose today to take a different route.

But I wasn't alone, in any sense. Tibby and I had been married for fifteen years, and now seemed to go through life as a unit. We may have even seemed insular to our friends, but it was just that we were confident in our knowledge of each other, a self-reliant couple. How could I have failed to wonder, at that critical time, whether Tibby's choice would have been the same as mine? That's what I would go back to find out, at least to feel right about myself for having asked the question.

* * *

I can't remember a time when I didn't know I was adopted. My parents decided to tell me the simpler facts of my birth as soon as they thought I could understand. Until I was ten, my curiosity had not reached beyond those simple facts. That was about to change as my mother sat at her dressing table one evening, carefully applying makeup and only half-listening to my familiar questions.

The ritual began again as I stood watching Mom put on eye shadow. I was fidgeting around the room looking for ways to entertain myself while she rushed to get ready for a dinner party. She leaned into the mirror, chin tilted up, face just inches from the glass, her lips pursed in concentration as she applied the mascara brush to her lashes.

I made a twisted face in the mirror and, out of boredom, asked the question my mother had heard many times before: "Mommy, when did you see me for the first time?"

She sighed, knowing that we were starting an old conversation again, but her soft Virginia accent hid any impatience she may have felt. "Honey, we saw you a few days after you were born, in the maternity ward at the hospital." I never asked about my birth parents, the missing faces in the maternity ward. They didn't seem to fit into the story I wanted to hear.

"What did I look like?" I stumbled around the room, pretending that I was a peg-legged pirate, not really thinking much about the question.

"Oh, you were the most beautiful, little pink baby. All the nurses said so, too."

"What did you do when you saw me for the first time?"

"I asked when I could hold you." She pulled her crossed arms to her chest, as if cradling me once again for the first time, her hands still holding the momentarily forgotten mascara brush and case.

We had gone through the standard questions and answers up to this point. Children seem to find comfort in repetitiveness, asking the same questions and expecting the same answers, just as they listen to the same bedtime stories until their parents no longer need the books to recite the lines. But this time I asked a question that hadn't been on my mind until the moment I asked it: "Mommy, why didn't they want to keep me?" I stopped playing aimlessly with the coins on Dad's bedside table and turned all of my attention to my mother.

I would have been satisfied with any answer, but my mother didn't push the question aside. She twisted around slowly on the upholstered bench and looked at me cautiously. "David, I'm sure they wanted to keep you. They just couldn't." The strain in her voice made it sound like she was pleading with me to accept what she was saying. "They were a young married couple. They were struggling to get by and wanted a better home for you than they thought they could give you. Their other son…." She drew in her breath and turned back to stare at herself in the mirror, as if trying to see in her face what to do next.

I was studying her face in the mirror, too. She glanced at me self-consciously and saw that I understood what she had let slip.

"Oh, dear." Tears pooled in her eyes; her shoulders sagged. "I didn't want you to find out like this." She paused, resigning herself to finishing the interrupted sentence. "They already had another little boy when you were born. We were told that he was seven years old and had a lot of medical problems."

The idea rolled over me in a warm wave of excitement: I had a

brother! My mother may have seen shock on my face, but it was fas-
cination, my eyes focusing on nothing while I considered this strange
new concept. She may have wanted to save me from agonizing over
why my birth parents would keep one kid and not another, but that
wasn't on my mind. I was completely absorbed by the raw appeal of
having a big brother, a chance to hope for something I hadn't even
imagined in the past. But I acted as if the news was a minor curiosity,
withdrawing into myself to figure out what I thought.

* * *

My parents had been guarded with outsiders about my adoption
when I was growing up, and that seemed natural back then. Adoption
was not an open topic for polite society, and I had grown up thinking
that there was a stigma to it. I still remember my parents' shock, and
my sense of betrayal, when I was described in one of my dad's office
newsletters as their teenaged *adopted* son.

As an adult I hadn't worked so hard at secrecy, but "adopted" was
not one of the labels I used to describe myself to others. Those labels
would necessarily have included "Washington lawyer," the career choice
that defined me against my will after fifteen years in big law firms. I
had been hunched over my desk at the office when Tibby called about
my look-alike on the D.C. subway.

My wife's whisper sounded conspiratorial. I could picture her
talking into the phone with her hand cupped around the mouthpiece.
"I told her, 'No,' you didn't have a brother, but I asked her where she
saw him. She thinks he got on at the Falls Church station but he was
still on the train when she got off at Farragut West. I asked her as many
questions as I could without acting too strange." It was easier for Tibby
to say "no" than to give the more complicated answer.

I had turned away from the legal document glaring at me on the
computer screen, caught up in her words. "Do you think it's possible

the guy is sitting at a desk a few blocks from here, working on something just as boring as I am?" I pushed the phone tighter to my ear as I swiveled away from the desk and stood up to look, blindly, out the office window. The cord tightened, tugging the phone across the desk as I pressed my forehead to the glass. Could this possibly be the day that I found my brother, or at least a fresh trail to him?

* * *

I had tried from the very first day onward to imagine what my brother would be like. He would have been seven years older than me, if my mother had the facts right. Our age difference would have made my brother and me unlikely co-conspirators if we had grown up in the same house. But in those early days, when the idea of my unexpected brother was so fresh, my kid fantasies were that we looked and acted a lot alike, even if most of the real brothers I knew didn't. We would have been best friends.

My fantasies were uncomplicated and idealistic, just as childhood fantasies should be. In real life, I was already beginning to see myself as out of step with the world around me. I was sure that my brother would have helped me understand how to fit in, easing my morning terrors as I walked to elementary school.

The school was on the edge of a neighborhood that hadn't existed three years before. My route was a muddy path through undeveloped fields, along an old barbed-wire fence intended to keep in the bony Florida cows whose hooves had carved the rut in the first place. The cows were long gone, and their path would soon be replaced by a road running from one assembly-line housing project to the next.

I scuffed along the path, banging my tin lunch box against each fence post and trying to work out how to slow my progress toward the torture chamber without being late for the bell. I was so good at worrying that I could build my fears around two mutually exclusive objectives; disaster awaited whether or not I got to school on time.

The prevailing smell intensified my misery as I walked: The janitor fired up the incinerator on the edge of the schoolyard as his first task each morning, pushing yesterday's trash into the flames. The humid Florida air filled with the smell of the burning stale milk that coated the insides of all those wax-paper cartons forced on us in the cafeteria at lunchtime.

My brother would have been with me on those walks to school, emotionally if not physically. He would have shown me how to fit in where I didn't think I belonged, would have been the confident force behind me proving that life was easier than I feared. I wouldn't have noticed the nauseating stench in the damp morning air. It all would have been better somehow.

All those years later I stood with my forehead against the window glass in my office, looking more at my own reflection than the street scene outside. I wanted to find my brother.

2

It seemed like a good time to start chasing my brother's shadow. I was approaching my fortieth birthday and had long since lost enthusiasm for the practice of law, the activity that swallowed most of my waking hours. Early on, my career choice had rewarded my perfectionism; when practiced well, the law was a nitpicker's game, full of details to trip you up if ignored. The job otherwise left me aching for creativity in my life. I was at just the point when I could use an interesting detour.

I needed to find my brother one day, probably long after my birth parents had died, but what if he was right here, right now? What if I continued to hedge my emotions, refusing to admit how much I really wanted to find him, only to discover years later that he had worked around the corner from my law firm but had drifted away before I began the search? Or that he had died while I made excuses? It was time to accept the risk that I might not find what I was looking for, or that I would be rejected when I did.

I was warming to the idea of learning more about my birth parents as well. I had never allowed them to be part of my fantasies in the past. They hadn't wanted me, so I had ignored them in return.

It was safer to pretend that I didn't need to find my birth family, so I hid behind another reason to justify the search: Just when my fantasy brother may have sat down across from Motty on the subway car, I had been suffering through months of medical tests for an elusive problem whose diagnosis could have been made obvious by my family medical history, if I'd only had access to the information. The reality was that my thyroid had shut down, leaving me exhausted by a slow metabolism. I didn't fit the doctors' stereotype of the older women who usually came in with that problem, so the correct diagnosis (and its easy treatment) wasn't on their minds. Ignoring the obvious had led to increasingly exotic and pessimistic theories.

By the time the doctors had dragged me through the possibility of a rare brain tumor, with delayed testing results to prolong the terror, the need for a biological past had become my new excuse for finding my birth family. I could point to all those times I sat in a doctor's reception room filling out the new-patient forms. I always had to scribble "adopted" across the section that asked for my parents' medical history. It simplified and complicated things at the same time. That one word was a complete answer to all of the questions, but it made the doctor's job that much harder. I had no clues to my past and the doctor had none to my hereditary weaknesses.

* * *

Tibby's strong mental image of my brother also helped to nudge me into the search. She had been sautéing onions for dinner the night the doctor had called to say that I wasn't dying of a brain tumor. I was chopping carrots, the little stuff that let me pretend to do my share of the cooking.

The reprieve had put Tibby into a reflective mood. It was good news, but a reminder of the fragile mortality that was an unstated theme while we waited for the test results. She spoke without turning away from the stove. "What do you think he looks like?" We had gotten used to understanding each other's context-divorced questions. I knew she was talking about my brother. He had been one of many diversionary topics that week.

"Got me. If I had seen Motty's guy on the train, I probably wouldn't have given him a second look."

"Like when people say you look like Rock Hudson or Christopher Reeve?"

I laughed derisively. "And who were some of the other ones? Alan Alda? Or is it just that I'm supposed to sound like him?" I had to admit that, whenever I heard my recorded voice, there was a bit more of the wry Alda to my tone than I would have liked. I didn't want to hear myself coming off as elitist or cynical.

I self-consciously tried not to sound like Alan Alda as I kept on. "Do you actually think, standing next to them, I would look enough like any of those guys that somebody would say we looked like brothers? And how many brothers actually look that much like brothers, anyway?"

"Well, Motty said he was tall and elegant, just like you. She described his Italian suit. She even said he acted like you, kind of above the crowd."

I winced. "Like snobby?"

"No, like impervious to the masses on the subway." She laughed, pairing her words with a chin tilted upward.

"'Course, doesn't everybody say we've started to look and act alike, just like people and their dogs? And you're the 'Pup', so I must be the master." I had many, ever-changing nicknames for Tibby, most of them nonsensical. "Pup" and "Pip" seemed to be the least curious ones I allowed myself to use in front of other people. "Be careful," I scolded. "You might just be describing yourself."

Suddenly I grabbed my wife around her trim waist and started the maneuver that shocked our mothers whenever (infrequently) they saw it: I lifted Tibby two feet off the floor and began to swing her upside-down. It always seemed to amuse her, so she would stiffen to attention, making herself an inert object that was easier to lift. I shook her up and down, gently, while pretending that she was being punished for her impudence. After reversing the process and returning her safely to the ground, I ended the performance with: "Now that you've been punished, have you learned the error of your ways?"

She pushed her short brown hair back into place and smoothed out her blouse, pretending that her dignity had been destroyed. Then she gave me the look that also shines from the grainy, black-and-white photo that's always on my desk: The three-year-old Tibby is standing on the concrete edge of a pond in the center of a Chilean town, the string in her hand running down to a toy sailboat bobbing in the water, a little girl staring at the camera with a smile that is strangely shy and devilish at once.

* * *

Tibby wanted the sighting of my older twin to be true, even if she was just as doubtful as I was that the subway rider could be my brother. She thought my brother would be everything I was, only older and wiser. He would be a strong influence on me, helping to hone my better instincts while sanding down my rough edges.

Tibby's father had died suddenly when she was a young teenager. I had heard many stories about the talented and enthusiastic man she so clearly loved as both father and friend. She strongly believed that he and I would have enjoyed each other's company, and I would have liked the opportunity to see whether she was right. I suspect that she had used some of her father's qualities to paint a mental picture of my brother.

Tibby poured chicken stock into the pan of onions. "You know my theory on growing older."

"That we shouldn't do it?"

"That, too," she nodded. "But I think we just become more of whatever we really are. A jerk just becomes more of one. We lose the ability to hide our best and worst traits. Whatever's at the core gets concentrated."

"Doesn't sound too promising for me," I responded with a wince. Tibby had had to stand by more than once, waiting for my latest red-faced tirade to come to an end. She knew that I took everything too personally, suffering no transgression easily and holding everyone to impossible standards of conduct.

"Of course it does, my love," she countered. "I think your brother's going to be like you: smart and curious about life. He's going to have done interesting things, and he'll want to tell you all about them."

I laughed. She sounded like a little girl playing make-believe. She chose the words carefully to describe her hopes for my brother, real-izing that a wish list of his sterling qualities might sound like a reverse catalog of my deficiencies. I liked hearing her optimistic theories, even if I would have been satisfied with a lesser man than she imagined. Maybe that's why I wasn't quite as disappointed as she was with how things turned out.

3

"Pope & Pope. May I help you?" The woman's voice was cheery, not like the icy tone of the receptionists at my big-city law firm. Her strong Virginia accent was both distinctive and comforting to me. Most of my maternal relatives were from Virginia, where I had spent summers and holidays as a kid.

"Yes, my name is David Ford. Could I speak to Tanner Pope, please?" I forced myself to keep my voice even, trying to hide my nervousness over what I hoped to accomplish. I had already checked out the firm's listing in a legal directory and knew that the Richmond lawyer I wanted had died four years before; his name and dates of birth and death were carried on the masthead as a memorial to the founder of the firm. It may have been disingenuous, but I thought it would be easier to get what I wanted if they had to be the bearers of bad news: Poor guy. The lawyer he's so anxious to talk to is dead.

The receptionist paused, then spoke softly, as if it might come as a shock to me: "I'm sorry, sir. Mr. Pope died in 1989. But his son is a lawyer here. Would you like to speak to him?"

"Oh, my. I'm very sorry to hear that." I thought my disappointment sounded sincere. "It would be great if I could talk to his son. Thanks." I wouldn't have been all that surprised even if I hadn't researched the law firm. Tanner Pope was the attorney who had handled my private adoption nearly four decades before. He had separately interviewed both sets of my parents, two couples matched up by the obstetrician who was about to deliver me. Those interviews were the closest the couples would ever come to meeting each other.

The hold-button silence was broken by a man's voice. "This is Richard Pope."

"I, uh, hello. My name's David Ford." My confidence seemed to have deserted me in an instant. "I'm a lawyer in Washington, D.C., but I'm calling on…a, uh, personal matter." Was I trying to show that I should be taken seriously?

Pope seemed to realize that I needed help getting started. "Terry says you were hoping to speak to my father. Is there something I can do for you instead, Mr. Ford?" You might be able to do a lot for me, I thought to myself, if I could just get back to playing the self-assured lawyer and ask focused questions. I cradled the phone between my left ear and shoulder and wiped my damp palms down my pants legs.

"Um, my mother gave me your father's name. He represented my parents in my adoption." It was a new experience to feel awkward talking to another lawyer. I spent my life talking to lawyers, but could barely control my breathing as I sat bent over my desk, my face almost resting on the blotter as I talked into the phone. "Mom said he might be able to help me find my birth parents, or really my medical history…." I was rambling, not wanting to get to the end of the sentence, the point where the lawyer might tell me to get lost.

I stopped talking. Silence filled the phone line. Richard Pope was gearing up to face another anxious adoptee. Did he already understand that I wanted a lot more than stale medical history out of his father's files?

Pope cleared his throat. "Mr. Ford, if you had called before my father passed away, he would have invited you down for a visit and told you he wouldn't be able to help you." He sounded about my age, with the same sort of serious tone I tried to enforce in my first contacts with new clients. I can sometimes be too quick with irreverence that skirts a bit close to the line in iffy situations, but I was learning to be more deliberate about what came out of my mouth. I had embarrassed myself a few times with comments that had seemed clever before I said them.

This lawyer wasn't going to engage me in witty banter. "Dad would have tried his best to convince you to leave things as they are. Maybe he would have succeeded. He was a persuasive man." Pope paused, as if lost momentarily in a private memory. "You would have enjoyed the conversation, even if he refused to give you what you wanted."

"I can be persuasive, too." My words sounded feeble. I don't know whether I was trying to convince Pope or myself that I intended to get what I wanted.

"I'm sure you can. Here's the thing: My dad grew up in an orphanage. Aside from his regular law practice, he performed hundreds of private adoptions to help other kids avoid his fate. He felt strongly that the information in his files was confidential to both sets of parents and should not be revealed unless everybody was okay with it. It was his way of making sure that the system kept working and protected all the conflicting interests."

Pope had begun to speak more quickly; his tone became more relaxed, as if he were about to speak for himself rather than his father. The son was going to violate the father's principles.

"But I have a different view than he did about providing information to our adoptees. I feel that this firm represented the adoptive parents who retained us. We'll dig up your files, which may take a few days. In the meantime, if your adoptive parents get me a letter authorizing the release of the files, I'll send them right out."

I sat at my desk, tapping my fingers on the arms of my chair. Should I let myself enjoy what I had just heard over the phone? If the file contained half of what Richard Pope expected from past expeditions into his father's records, I would soon know a lot about my birth family. As the call was ending, I had asked hesitantly: "Will the file include the names of my birth parents?" I shook my head at the almost child-like tone I used to ask the question. I was so afraid of the wrong answer that my common sense had left me. For all kinds of reasons, legal and practical, the lawyer's files *had* to include the names of two people who sat across the desk from him to discuss giving up their unborn child.

Pope answered with surprise in his voice: "Of course." He left off the "you idiot" part. I could almost see him raising his eyebrows, wondering if I really was the lawyer I said I was. Lawyers assume that other lawyers are smart; it's one of the profession's many arrogances. But he wasn't hearing a lot of brilliant reasoning from my end of the line. Maybe he was accustomed to the fractured, emotional thinking of adoptees in search of their origins.

∗ ∗ ∗

In my own defense there was precedent from my past for worrying that I might get documents with lots of information but none that would lead me any closer to finding my birth parents. A decade before, I had come across a magazine article about how states took widely different approaches to disclosing adoption records. Virginia, where I was born, appeared willing to give its adoptees some access to their files. I called the state agency and two days later spoke to a social worker who held my file in her hands. I wanted to crawl through the telephone and stare over her shoulder.

"What kinds of documents are in the file?" The veins in my neck pulsed to my racing heartbeat.

"They're probably not going to be as informative as you'd like," she answered. "Mostly bureaucratic paperwork, reports of home visits to your adoptive parents before and after your birth." Her tone sounded like she had had too many of these conversations with adopted children looking for answers.

"Do the records show my birth parents' names?"

"Yes, sir. We aren't permitted to give out that information. As

I said, we can send you a copy of the file, but it will have your birth parents' names removed."

I had heard that sympathetic clerks sometimes bent the rules, but this woman didn't sound like the type. I didn't have the nerve to push the issue over the phone. "If my birth parents had ever contacted the state to say that they would like to hear from me, would the file show that?"

"Yes, it probably would," she said. Then, silence.

"My file doesn't show that, does it?"

"No, sir. I'm sorry." This time she did sound sorry.

I would discover that the social worker may have been more sympathetic than I thought. But first the file had to be delivered through what sounded like a patronizing process, including a face-to-face interview at the corresponding agency in Maryland, where I lived.

Nine days later, I sat in a molded plastic chair in the waiting area of a drab government building. The chair was orange and bouncy, the kind that seemed to populate every government office building and no place else. I tapped the side of my shoe rapidly against the worn linoleum floor, wanting to get on with what I expected to be an aggravating exercise. I was alone in the room, so I didn't have to hide my impatience.

The buzz of an electronic lock startled me as a baby-faced bureaucrat noisily pulled the door open. "Mr. Ford?" She sang the question in a kindergarten-sugary tone, adding what sounded like three extra syllables in the process.

"That's me." I tried to match her glee without sounding like I was mocking her.

"Please come right this way." She held the door open and gave me a big smile, as if to assure me that everything was going to be all right. I wanted to tell her that her time would be better spent trying to help those who really needed it, but thought that I could speed the process by keeping my mouth shut. After what seemed like two circuits around the building, down corridors indistinguishable from one another, she interrupted her string of idle chatter to point me into a room where more of the orange chairs flanked a heavy folding table.

The young social worker offered me a cup of water from a dented, steel pitcher, then turned her attention to the manila envelope that she had squared in front of her on the table. "So what do we have here?"

She turned to look at me. After a moment of silence, I realized that the question wasn't rhetorical, that she actually wanted me to tell her what we had here.

"Um, I think those are my adoption records from Virginia. At least that's what I'm here to get."

"And what do you hope to learn from the records?" she asked.

"Not much, probably," I shrugged. "The lady I spoke to at the Virginia agency told me it was mostly bureaucratic paperwork. I've had some medical problems that I'm trying to figure out, not that those," pointing toward the envelope, "are likely to give me much insight. Every little bit of information helps, though, right?"

"Perhaps." Now Miss Kindergarten tried to add a few years to her voice. "Sometimes these kinds of records send people down the wrong path. We don't want to see you get hurt."

"Thanks for your concern, but I think I can handle it." I paused and gave her my most serious, lawyerly stare. "This is not an emotional event for me." At least it won't be in front of you, I thought.

She returned my stare for a moment, then pushed the envelope across the table toward me. I picked it up and, turning it over, was surprised to see that its flap was still sealed. I began to slide my finger under the flap, then stopped. I didn't want to share the event, so I quickly thanked the social worker, stood up, and headed for the door.

"Wait, sir. Wouldn't you like me to be there for you?" She seemed honestly concerned for me, but I wanted to be alone with my past.

"No thanks. I've taken enough of your time."

"But…." I was already out the door, heading down the first of all those long, gray corridors.

* * *

The summer heat had concentrated in the interior of my tiny black sports car. I started the engine, cranked up the air, and looked at the dashboard clock, which showed that I had already been out of the office for too long. Sticky with sweat, I loosened my tie and stared at the envelope resting against the steering wheel in my lap. I turned it over, finished my finger-slide under the flap, and pulled out the shiny photocopies from microfilmed archives. I fanned through the slick sheets of paper, surprised to see that nearly every page had tiny, rectangular holes in it where someone had laboriously razored out each identifying reference to my birth parents.

I expected names to be blacked out, not physically gone from the page. But the process had been imperfect. I attacked the pages with my lawyer's eye for detail and caught the error on my second pass. There on one of the last pages was my birth family's name where a hole should have been: Jones. Was it an oversight or the clerk's subversive clue? Jones was such a common name; I wondered if it was a pseudonym, like "Doe," just another officious protocol. If that was the case, though, it didn't seem likely that they would have worked so hard to obscure an alias in the files.

I studied the pages over the next week. Most of the file was taken up with formalistic court pleadings needed for my adoption, but the first document in the stack was an investigator's report titled: "In re: Adoption of Baby Boy [Jones]." That's who I was to the judicial process, "Baby Boy Jones," except that "Jones" had been replaced by a hole in the paper I held in my hand. I pushed around the idea of this alternative last name, imagining myself going through life with a different label.

For an adopted kid, a name seemed little more than a territorial, rather than hereditary, link to the people who had given it to you. Your adoptive name was evidence of a claim staked, a border defined. It was hard to get excited about the exploits of distant generations of relatives with whom you had no blood tie. It didn't seem to make much difference that some great-great-grandfather had survived a potato famine somewhere, or that his offspring continued a chain of events ending with you coming sideways into the family history.

It entertained me to think of myself as a Jones once in a while. From the day I saw my birth name in print, I rarely failed to ask any Joneses I met a few of the "where-ya-from" kinds of questions. If any of them were from central Virginia, I sometimes asked more.

Near the end of the investigator's typed report on the subject of Baby Boy Jones, a paragraph captioned "Separation from the natural parents" confirmed the story my mother had told me all those years before:

> The child was born to a married couple, both of whom were thirty-two years of age. They have one child who is reported to be seven years old. The father is employed as a safety engineer. The parents did not believe they could support the child adequately and provide for him in the way which they desired.

I reread the paragraph many times, finding satisfaction in a childhood story's confirmation. It looked like I might have a brother after all. A twelve-word sentence was enough to make him seem real for the first time.

The investigator's hand-written notes were in the file as well. She quoted herself as saying to my birth parents that she was "puzzled also as to why they wanted to give up the child," in light of their obvious intelligence, "college educ., etc." My birth parents apparently were not ready to talk. The final report said, in what feels like an archaically civilized tone, that the Joneses "had referred the visitor"—the word "visitor" conjuring up the unlikely picture of a Sunday afternoon in the parlor—"to the adoption attorney, as they believed he had the necessary information." That sounded like a nice way of saying that my birth parents had told the investigator to shut up and get out of their house.

I wished that the investigator had been more than "puzzled" about my birth parents' decision, at least enough to press them for better answers. But she wouldn't have shared my intense interest in the topic, and I hadn't known then what tough opponents my birth parents could be. The most dedicated bureaucrat might have decided that it wasn't worth the effort to keep trying to pin them down.

The investigator didn't learn the interesting parts of the story. If she had discovered the truth about them, my birth parents probably would have been subjected to a much more intrusive scrutiny.

At least these dry court papers were evidence that some of my doubts had been wrong. I had wondered whether my older brother might be a myth, and the uncertainty had made it easier to do nothing to find him.

The adoption file was the first tangible evidence of my birth, certainly more than the embossed birth certificate stating that I was the son of my adoptive parents. The certificate reflected a fiction of sorts, as if my birth parents had never existed. The adoption file in my hands reflected the truth, or at least what my birth parents were offering as the truth at the time.

4

T he state records had shown me the first glimpse of my brother—but not much more. My birth parents' newly discovered last name was hopelessly common, so it was a weak lead. My brother really existed, although his image was no clearer to me. And the state investigator couldn't understand why I was being given up for adoption. The poorly photocopied papers were already beginning to curl and yellow as I stuck them back into their manila envelope and down into a file drawer, where they would be ignored for a long time.

It would take me a half-dozen years to make that call to Richard Pope. The file that he was about to send me would not be so obscure as my official adoption records or as easy to put aside. I was uneasy about asking my parents to send the authorization letter Pope had requested. Mom had given me the adoption lawyer's name months before, so she and Dad knew I might try to contact him. But they didn't know any more than I had about what would happen *if* I actually went looking for the lawyer.

I can't explain why it had taken me so long to get to this point. It was such a simple thing to pick up the phone and dial the number that I easily found in the legal directory. I was ordinarily impatient, prone to quick action and critical of those who weren't. But if I did nothing to find my birth family, everything was still possible. There would be no dead ends, no ugly answers to the questions I had.

I called Mom and told her about the call. "He was very nice and said all I needed to do was get your written authorization."

"That's wonderful, David." I could hear genuine happiness in her voice. I had thought she would be pleased for me, even if she worried about what finding my birth family might do to our relationship. "What should the letter say?"

"The words aren't important. You just need to say it's okay to give me the files." Mom always fretted over details, sometimes asking questions about nuances that seemed indistinguishable to me. I tried to control my exasperation in responding to the multiple variations on whatever question was on her mind at that moment.

This time I knew my mother had a right to treat the letter to the lawyer as an important document. It felt like the first step in a chain reaction whose result couldn't be predicted. She had to have some anxiety. I did.

I reconsidered my quick answer to my mother's question, then asked: "Do you have a pen and paper nearby? I'll dictate what it should say, just a few sentences." I could hear her rustling in a drawer under the phone for a pen and something to write on. "Take your time, Mom." I was paying guilty penance for my impatience.

I asked her to send the letter directly to Richard Pope. The photocopy I got in the mail showed that I was right about how she viewed the letter. Mom is a versatile artist, her skills having been broadened by a long career as a public school art teacher. The letter displayed her talent for calligraphy to the fullest; it looked more like a certificate of merit than the simple statement that it was supposed to be.

*　*　*

Two weeks after I spoke with Richard Pope, his envelope arrived with no more ceremony than was shown to all the other stuff shoved through our mail slot at home. Seeing the package in the pile on the floor felt like those other big events that got announced by gloriously thick or painfully thin envelopes—college acceptances and rejections,

SAT scores, and bar admission results. They all changed the future in ways that shouldn't have been reduced to a few sheets of paper.

By then, Pope had summarized the information in the files for me over the telephone, but nothing he said had prepared me for the chill of holding copies of the forty-year-old documents in my hands. I skimmed the half-inch stack of paper, trying to get a quick measure of it, just as I routinely did whenever a complex legal document first hit my desk. This time, instead of swearing to myself about what the fool on the other side had done to screw up the deal, I smiled at the contents of a lawyer's file from another era. I would have been a little curious about it even if it hadn't been my pre-natal biography.

The documents had sat in storage, untouched for decades, before being handed over to the one person who cared the most about seeing them. Tanner Pope must have understood their value to someone like me, even if he would have prevented this moment from happening if he had been alive. I wonder if, late in life, he would have destroyed his many adoption files if he had anticipated his son's decision to reveal their contents.

I was still standing in the hallway of our house, torn envelope tucked under one arm as I shuffled through Pope's papers, too absorbed to move away from the open front door. I called out to Tibby to tell her what the mail had brought as I finally wandered toward the kitchen, still reading as I went, and then spread out the documents on the counter for both of us to study. The kitchen counter was my wife's impromptu filing cabinet for all the bits of paper that interested her: loosely formed piles of recipes, magazine articles about art and places to visit, and books to be read. I shoved several piles aside to make room for our newest project, the first of many times that her interests would be pushed crudely out of the way to accommodate my birth family.

The centerpiece of the file was the old lawyer's scribbled notes of his interviews with both sets of parents. My hands shook as I strained to decipher his handwriting. The pages roared with the full names of my birth parents, my brother, and both sets of grandparents, the address of my parents at the time I was born, and other, almost random, facts about their lives. The name "Jones" wasn't the alias that I had worried it might be; there it was in the lawyer's own hand.

I tried to detach myself from the emotion of the moment as I studied the documents, hoping to draw every bit of useful information out of them as quickly as possible. This seemed like the time to get the most out of my training as a lawyer, rather than just to paw excitedly through the pages.

Tanner Pope's notes suggested that he had wanted to provide factual context for the people sitting across the desk from him. As I read and re-read the papers in the file, I wondered what it would have felt like in that position, deciding what questions to ask the birth parents and which answers to give to the adoptive ones. The notes gave me a sense of intimacy for the proceedings, as if I had been a silent observer at the interviews of two sets of my soon-to-be parents.

The notes were informal, meant only to remind the lawyer of what sanitized generalities to offer the adoptive parents when he met them later. Tanner Pope never intended for me to be struggling to make sense of them, and I felt a trespasser's guilt as I nearly memorized them. I suspect that he would have done things differently if he had known I would be reading his words. I know that I would have asked him to do a few things differently as he pursued my unborn interests. My questions, at least the ones I would like answered now, would be far more pointed than the lawyer's professional decorum would have permitted.

Pope would have been about the age I am now as he sat with my parents. I could empathize with how he would have felt about someone reading his private notes, taken in haste and without expecting that anyone else would be scrutinizing every word. I couldn't always understand my own notes and would have squirmed at the idea of exposing them to someone else's judgment, especially an adoptee with so much invested in the words.

Deciphering the lawyer's longhand, I read that my birth parents had been living in a rented apartment around the corner from the church my adoptive family had attended for a generation in Richmond. His scribbles said that my birth mother had a much older sister and that my birth father had a twin sister as well as an older sister. There were short lists of relatives' names and general health conditions. Much of it seems meaningless today but must have been a 1950s lawyer's effort to preserve a medical history. What could my adoptive parents or I have done with the fact that my birth father's sister's health was "good?"

A section of the notes seemed more like dictation—hurried writing capturing a monologue—than responses to specific questions the lawyer might have asked. I guessed that my birth mother wanted to describe her family history in glamorous detail, as if to show she wasn't just another tramp giving up a baby. She had been through "business school and high school—never below 6th in her class," said Pope's scrawl. She had worked as the secretary to the math department at the Virginia Military Institute in her hometown, Lexington. My birth father attended Washington & Lee University, the other college in town, for two years. He was described as "highly intelligent—speaks Chinese and Spanish," but it's unclear whether Tanner Pope was recording his own observations about the man I assume was sitting in front of him, or merely keeping up with his interviewee's commentary. Based on the rhythm of the lawyer's note-taking, I pictured my birth mother, not her husband or the lawyer, as the force driving the interview. Whether my Sherlock Holmes deductions were right or wrong is anybody's guess; I was simply trying to apply my legal training to the thin evidence in front of me.

At the end of the interview, or at least at the end of his notes, Pope recorded his own assessment of my birth parents' physical attributes: My father's height—a shocking six feet eleven inches—beat mine by seven inches. I didn't think *anybody* was that tall back then. (The lawyer's note was a misprint for six feet one inch, but I didn't know that then.) After noting my birth father's "hair dark—eyes brown" and my mother's "green eyes—dark hair," Pope had scrawled "nice features" next to each of their sketchy descriptions. Not much to use in summoning up a mental picture, I thought.

Why had I been given up for adoption? Pope only wrote: "Financial burden too great—do not want the child to go through Welfare." That was the same, skeletal answer that my mother had passed on to me all those years before and that appeared in the state adoption records. I was given up for adoption as a matter of simple household economics. I wanted the answer to be more complicated than that. My ego still wasn't ready to accept such a cold rationale. The lawyer's notes weren't going to get me any closer to the facts.

Pope didn't mention other things that Mom remembered from her meeting with the lawyer. He had told my future parents that my brother had serious health problems at birth that required major, expensive surgery and that my paternal grandfather was in failing health and in need of a nursing home. But there was no indication in the notes that an aging parent and a sick kid had forced my birth parents' decision. It seemed a thin explanation that this married, seemingly intelligent couple, with just that one other kid, was so taxed that they couldn't keep their family together. How were they so different from other families trying to make ends meet in Eisenhower's America?

Remembering that the state investigator had been perplexed as well, I felt justified in second-guessing the merits of my birth parents' claimed hardships. I wanted my birth parents to be better than selfish and weak. Or maybe I was afraid that those traits fell a little too close to my own when it came to taking responsibility for others. Was it meaningless irony that Tibby and I had never made room for children in our own marriage?

The lawyer's notes also answered less important questions raised by my mother's recitations of the sketchy facts she had about my birth family. I really was the direct descendant of a pre-Civil War-era governor of Virginia, whose last name was repeated as my birth mother's maiden name. A real name, not just a vague reference to some ancient governor, made it easier to buy the story that Mom had told me even before she had let slip that I had a brother. I had been cynical about the claim to such a distinguished lineage. It had seemed unlikely to me that an adopted kid would find himself at the end of an old Virginia line. At the same time, the Governor let me see that, whether or not my birth parents and brother would embrace me if I found them, I could explore a relationship with a larger family than just the people who had given me up. I was as much the Governor's legacy as any other blood relative.

Judging from Pope's notes, my birth parents tried to convey the significance of my heritage. It might have been an effort to show a degree of merit they were afraid wouldn't otherwise be apparent, but even then they were offering information that they wouldn't have wanted me to learn. They wanted the lawyer's respect, not mine.

5

I t was easier to find my great-great-great-grandfather than my birth parents. It was also less risky; he was an appealing abstraction, a temporary stand-in for the descendants I was chasing. The Honorable Henry Alexander Wise (1806–1876) was a U.S. congressman, an ambassador to Brazil, governor of Virginia, and— most important to die-hards below the Mason-Dixon Line—a brigadier general in the Confederate Army. He was the subject of a serious academic work, whose author described the governor as eccentric and incomprehensible. I joked with Tibby that I should claim Wise as a hereditary excuse for at least a few of the unattractive adjectives that might stick to me.

Governor Wise's ancestors had settled on the Eastern Shore of Virginia 150 years before he was born. I liked to see myself as part of a three-century American story, to consider my place in the governor's line. I wondered if it would merit an asterisk on a genealogist's chart of the Wise family tree.

Henry Wise was Virginia's last pre-war governor. He had opposed secession from the Union but had later accepted his duty to serve the commonwealth in the Civil War. An ambivalent slaveholder himself, he had been an inconsistent politician on the subject of abolition.

As a young congressman, my ancestor developed a reputation for being quick to incite a duel with his opponents, although he apparently carried out the act only once, wounding his opponent. Wise filled his five terms in the House of Representatives with fiery speeches and emotional attacks. His most charitable biographers considered him the second most influential Virginian of his time (after the exalted Robert E. Lee) but couldn't overlook the erratic episodes that defined his career in national politics.

Exploring this first line of knowledge about my birth family enabled me to circle around the real task. It was all an intellectual exercise, an easy game to play without fear of being hurt by what I might learn if I pressed on. I was stalling, even if I would have denied it at the time.

I could hide behind my busy schedule and the uncertainty about what steps to take next in looking for people who probably didn't want to be found. And I could always trot out the excuse that I was worried about whether I had the right to drop uninvited into my birth family's lives. It was all true, but not powerful enough to stop someone more willing to accept any outcome, good or bad. I needed the best result and expected the worst. My pessimism let me shrug my shoulders in anticipated defeat. Why start something that isn't likely to turn out well?

* * *

Henry Wise helped me breach the high wall around my birth family. Now, beyond the old stories, I had forty-year-old facts from the lawyer's notes that could lead me more directly to my goal, if I stopped torturing myself over whether to use them. First, there were the practical issues to debate: The weakness of using my birth family's hopelessly common surname as the starting place for the search was amplified by the first names of my father, Daniel, and brother, Gregory. Dan and Greg Jones? Their names sounded like unimaginative aliases, not clues to my past. Then there were the harder questions: Was it fair to disrupt my birth parents' lives, assuming they were still alive? Did my brother even know I existed? Would he want to know?

I let my lawyer's skill at coming up with real and imagined issues dissuade me from taking any big steps. I went through the ridiculous effort, in those days before Internet search engines, of photocopying the pages of the local phone book that included hundreds of entries named "Gregory Jones" or "G. Jones" with an eye to weeding out the unlikely candidates for my subway-riding brother. "Let's see . . . can't be 'Jones, Gregory, Lt. Col.,' because Motty said he was wearing a suit and heading downtown." Even after my brilliant deductive reasoning, the list had only narrowed to a daunting forty or more, and I pictured myself as a bizarre telemarketer interrupting people in mid-dinner with cold calls for instant brotherhood.

The pages of phone listings went back into my dog-eared, two-inch-thick research file and were never consulted again. The folder seemed to become a graveyard for paper that defined me, or at least pieces of my past, without giving any real shape to my future. The file's bulk taunted me. I made a living out of devouring paper, massive deal documents and memoranda on ponderous legal issues, but I couldn't manage to manipulate this pile to my advantage.

Months had passed since I had gotten Pope's notes. This was 1994, and I had just moved from one big Washington law firm to another. I reluctantly followed one of my law partners to a place that seemed proud of its painfully formal, almost hostile, atmosphere. I would ask friends: "You work in a smoke-free office?" Pause. "You're lucky. I work in an *oxygen*-free office."

Whenever I was stuck riding in the elevator with the managing partner of the firm, I tormented the cadaverous man with overly cheery conversation. On those days when I attempted wit, panic would sweep across his face. I imagined the debate in his brilliant legal mind: "I believe this is what's known as a humorous interchange. What should I do now?" He was usually saved by the bell, as the elevator announced its arrival at his floor.

It hadn't taken me long to realize that I wouldn't be making a lot of friends in the firm's hallways, so I was surprised when one of my

zombie-like partners bumped into me and began what passed for conversation in the building. I was so grateful for any acknowledgment
from my new partners that I tried to find something of interest in what
the man had to say, even though I suspected that he didn't know my
name.

He was a litigator specializing in tedious administrative actions
before the Federal Energy Regulatory Commission. The associates in
the firm referred to working with this guy as "getting FERCed," rhyming
the second word with "jerked" but implying a more unpleasant fate.
I stretched for something to say to my hallway buddy, then lamely
offered up: "How's the FERC treating you these days?" Conversation
was not an art form here, and the litigator probably couldn't imagine a
more interesting topic anyway.

He rocked back on his heels and seemed to be counting ceiling tiles
as he spoke. Eye contact was also not a cherished skill at the firm. "Just
finished an unusual evidentiary hearing in front of the Commission.
Actually had the chance to put up facts that we uncovered through a
private investigator." My new best pal talked through his teeth, his lips
and jaw barely moving. I wondered whether that was why he chopped
off the beginnings of his sentences. Was it just too much effort to move
the muscles in his face?   He spoke to the wall as he wandered off:
"First time in my career I used a detective. Most interesting. Highly
recommend the investigator, if you ever have the need."

I trotted after him, slowing my pace as I reached his side. "Could
be useful sometime, I suppose," trying to mask my interest. "How do
I get in touch with him?" Maybe my brother Gregory, subway rider or
not, would be an easier target for a pro than he had been for me.

I walked back toward my office, staring at the name and number
I had jotted on my yellow legal pad. It would be easy to pick up the
phone that minute and call the investigator, but I was still hesitant.
Finding Governor Wise meant that I had a clearer picture of the fifth

generation behind me than of the first, my birth parents. It was time to start taking risks, to look for answers that I might not like, to commit to a daunting goal. I had thought I wanted to find my brother; now I needed the rest of the story.

* * *

Over the phone Kevin Holden sounded more like a quick-talking college kid than the stereotypical, gravel-voiced private detective. After all that we would go through together, I still only have an untested mental image of Holden. He was never more than a disembodied voice, but he seemed to know his universe well enough to impress a beginner like me.

"I've done hundreds of missing-person searches, which is pretty much what you're after." Holden was on familiar ground, confident in his expectations. "The key is: We gotta find your birth mother first, before we try to track down your brother. She's the only one we're sure knows you're her kid."

I interrupted. "I'm sure my birth father was at the lawyer's interview. He had to know." I had told Holden about Tanner Pope's notes.

The detective's answer was a clue to the complexities that lay ahead for me: "From my experience, we don't know for sure that guy was her husband or who he was. The world's not a happy place. Nothing personal, but your idea that you're the product of two married people just isn't likely. Most adoptees are the product of teen pregnancies, rape, incest, or infidelity." Holden would be wrong about the circumstances of my birth, but he was right about my naiveté.

I felt the urge to rise up and defend the birth parents I hadn't met. Here were people I only knew through a few pages of a lawyer's notes, but I wanted to tell Holden that he had them all wrong. I needed to be careful, though. Building people up to my high expectations had led to sharp disappointment, and I meted out stiff penalties for failure to satisfy my standards. The investigator seemed unlikely to let my hopes rise too high.

"Some other stuff you need to know up front." Holden seemed to have given this speech before. "It's weird how often the person you're looking for turns out to have died just before you find him. Even so, my clients usually get at least some of what they're looking for."

Holden wasn't finished with his gloomy list of what could go wrong. "Another thing: It usually takes almost no time at all to find anybody. But if it doesn't happen fast, it's gonna take a while. In your case, you got a decent amount of information for me to go with, but I wish we were starting with something easier than Dan Jones. At least your father's middle name—what was it, Cogsworth?—adds a little traction."

Unfortunately Holden's worst case played out. The next year was marked with his infrequent phone calls describing failed leads. My birth parents seemed to have disappeared from the public records—or never to have been there in the first place. There was no evidence that the Joneses ever did the obvious things like buy a house or car on credit or even apply for a credit card. It didn't dawn on Holden or me that they might have been trying to avoid leaving a trail. It probably shouldn't have; we had no reason to suspect that they had anything to hide, other than me. We didn't know it yet, but my birth parents had learned to function skillfully in two worlds: one, the open universe of a typical Baby Boom family living under their real names, and the other, the shuttered windows of a family with something to hide from prying eyes.

I had spent nearly forty years *not* looking for my birth family, but once I had taken these first steps, my impatience drove me to frustration. Hiring Holden was the right move, but now I had to wait for somebody else to make progress for me. My own efforts may have been ineffective, but relying on others wasn't my style.

I hated waiting in line for anything, and now I was standing in what felt like the longest line. I couldn't shake the image of my brother out there, taunting me in my imagination as he walked down the sidewalk in front of my building. He would have just come out of the Middle Eastern deli next door, a brown bag with his takeout sandwich in hand. It would be a cold, misty afternoon in October. He would have pulled the collar of his raincoat up around his ears and looked to the sky to guess whether it was going to start pouring before he could duck back into the lobby of his building around the corner. His eyes would have skimmed past the window of my fifth-floor office, unable to see me behind the reflection of the gray skies in the glass. Would I have seen him, scanned his face with sudden recognition, if I had just chosen that moment to look down at the street?

*   *   *

At the end of a year of waiting for good news from Holden, me pestering him every few months, I decided to act as my own junior detective again to chase some of the slim leads from the bits of information in the dead lawyer's interview notes. Holden had mentioned to me that the Holy Grail of missing person searches was a Social Security number, one item we didn't have for either of my birth parents. Maybe I could find one of those.

I called Holden, rushing my words when he picked up the phone. "Remember that Dan Jones supposedly attended Washington & Lee University?" Holden's silence challenged my urgency, and I forced myself into a slower tempo: "Should I drive down there and fake a reason to look over the shoulder of some registrar's assistant to see if I can spot a Social Security number?"

Holden laughed. "Like they're gonna have your father's fifty-year-old records lying around for you to play with? Look, I'm almost as frustrated as you are; this shouldn't be so tough. Before you try that on your own, I want to chase down one lead that's such a long shot I haven't bothered until now. We know from the lawyer's file that your birth father was in the Army in Korea. The Army records from back then were all destroyed in a St. Louis warehouse fire, but if he stayed in the reserves for a while after the war, there's a chance his records are somewhere else I can get access to. Don't expect too much out of this. If I can reach my contact, we'll know one way or the other pretty fast. Call you back."

"Kevin, I…." I heard a click and the dial tone. Good. My investigator was back on the job.

6

Under the best of circumstances I couldn't seem to sit still at my desk for more than minutes at a time. I had worked out a routine to keep myself from going insane: I would walk the circular hallway past all the other lawyers' offices on my floor, looking for any distraction to slow my return to my desk. I stopped at every water fountain along the way. Sometimes I would even take the grand stairway up a level or two just to pace another floor, even though it looked as sterile as the one I had just left. I had done this sort of drill in all of my law firms and was relieved that no one ever commented on my behavior.

I worried that I might look like a lifer plotting his escape from the prison exercise yard. I usually felt like one, and never more so than during the two hours it took for Holden to call me back. I couldn't even leave my office to pace while I waited for my secretary to announce the call from the investigator. Yvette didn't know who Holden was, beyond that he was someone whose calls I always took without once throwing any exasperated excuses at her for why I would need to call him back later.

She finally yelled from her station outside my door. "Kevin Holden on the line." It aggravated the lawyer next door that my secretary never used the intercom. I thought he needed an outlet for his bad temper, so I never discouraged Yvette's noisy habit.

Holden had told me not to hold my breath, but it felt like I hadn't exhaled for hours as I grabbed up the phone. I didn't have any pleasantries left in me: "So?"

"I can't believe it. It worked." He sounded as excited as I suddenly felt. So much for the cold professionalism he usually tried to convey. He had found Dan Jones's trail and had an old address for the man in southeastern Virginia. "Let me check it out before you get too excited." Too late for that, I thought, pushing my chair away from my desk and leaning back with my face aimed squarely to the ceiling.

I had no idea how long it might take for Holden to call again, but I considered myself officially off the billing clock until then. Nothing my clients needed would hold enough interest to keep me from fantasizing about what Holden might be learning. For all I knew, the investigator had promptly gone off to lunch, but he seemed wound up enough by the chase that I doubted he could wait any longer to find our elusive targets.

Twenty minutes later—did a minute suddenly have a thousand seconds to it?—Holden was on the phone again. This time his voice seemed another pitch higher. "Amazing," he announced, with more enthusiasm than I'd ever heard in his voice. "Your birth parents still live at the same address. I called their number. An older woman answered and I told her I was looking for my long-lost cousin Ernie Jones. I got a knack for talking to old ladies on the phone, especially when they're bored."

Holden kept going while I fought what felt like panic and tried to focus on every word. "She's definitely your mother. Everything fits. She's been married to Dan since the '40s...."

I stood up, kicking my chair away with the back of my leg. I stretched over my desk, one leg rising behind me, waving my right arm to get my secretary's attention across the hallway outside my open doorway. She looked up, her eye caught by the motion of my strange dance. I motioned for her to come over and shut my door. I didn't want anyone barging in. I dropped back into my chair, almost slipping off its front edge in the excitement.

Holden was still talking: "...and they lived in Richmond around the time you were born there."

"You got that kind of information out of her in one call?"

The investigator laughed, more a giggle that made him sound as giddy as I felt. "Look, I got a talent for this. Anyway, she's a really neat lady, real together and smart. She obviously cares about her family and is happy to talk about them. But here's the important stuff: You don't just have a brother."

He paused, heightening what he knew would be the drama in his next words. "You have two sisters."

"What?" It was the simplest of sentences, but made no sense to me. I stared at the blank page of the yellow legal pad in front of me on the desk, but no words appeared on it to help me interpret Holden's statement.

Holden was ready to move on, even if I wasn't. "Yeah. Probably should have anticipated something like that. I mean, *I* probably should have. Anyway, I think the sisters would be younger than you, the way she was talking."

Holden paused again; silence filled the space. "You still there, David?"

Two sisters? I shook myself back into focus. "Sorry. I hadn't anticipated that there were more after me." I tried to sound analytical, rather than mystified, keeping the sting out of my voice. But I didn't want there to be two sisters, just my brother. Was this some kind of insulting joke?

"What do you suppose that was all about?" I was probably directing the question more to myself than Holden. It was one thing to be the second and *last* child, given up by parents who had made a mistake and fixed it as well as they could. It was another to find yourself the odd man out of a family with three other kids.

"Who knows? Maybe they wanted girls." Holden laughed guiltily.

"Sorry. Bad joke." Maybe he wouldn't have laughed if he had known how I was taking the news: I had just been slapped by the birth parents I had never met.

I tried to recover, looking for information to distract my emotions. "Is there any doubt in your mind she's my mother?" Was this really how the search would end? It was already beginning to feel like the frightening excitement of a tire blowout at seventy miles an hour, followed by the adrenalin-fired struggle to get the car under control.

"None." Holden sounded like I was challenging his competence, rather than struggling to accept that I was so close to the end of the search. "Her husband is Daniel Cogsworth Jones. She's Sarah Jones. They've got a son seven years older than you named Gregory. They're the right ages. It all fits. Now you need to decide what you want to do next."

What I wanted to do next? There had to be a next, of course, but I was still tumbling in the present. "Let me talk to my wife." She would be a clearer thinker than I was at the moment, I thought. "But I guess the next step is to make some sort of direct contact." Tibby would be thrilled to hear that we had found my birth family, but what would she think about my two sisters? I hoped her first reaction would get me past mine. I should have been happier to find three siblings instead of just one.

Holden was oblivious to my turmoil. "I could have one of my female operatives call Sarah—a woman's voice is better for this kinda thing—and claim to be an administrative type from the hospital where you were born. She'll tell Sarah they've been contacted by someone claiming to be her child. Depending on how your mother reacts"—it felt odd for him to refer to a woman I didn't know as my mother—"my girl can offer to get you in touch with her or we can re-evaluate the situation. Of course, you could always call her yourself." His tone said that he didn't think that was such a good idea.

Whatever Holden thought, I couldn't imagine calling Sarah Jones. "No. She needs the opportunity to reject any contact. I'm trying to be fair here. I don't think I really have any right to do what we're about to do." That was a noble-sounding excuse for the truth: If I never made the next move, I could never be rejected by my birth family or, maybe worse, drawn into whatever trouble they might represent. I had heard enough stories about other adopted kids finding their wretched birth parents and then wishing they hadn't. People always trot out "nothing ventured, nothing gained" as justification for taking risk, but what about "nothing ventured, nothing lost?"

"David," Holden sighed, "you've come this far...."

"I'll call you back." I may have ended the call too abruptly, but I needed to talk it over with Tibby. She would keep me level.

* * *

I had been calling Tibby with updates on Holden's progress during the day. She would also have been struggling to concentrate on her work while waiting for the latest news. She had greater expectations than the ones I was willing to let anyone hear. I played down my hopes, not just for finding my birth family, but for most things in life. Expecting the worst, or at least not the best, meshed nicely with the practice of law; good lawyers are expected to help clients anticipate fall-back positions for risky business.

I often had in mind some sort of Plan B, a "what-if-it-doesn't-work" plan to soften personal failures, just as I did when working out a client's legal strategy. The simple act of coming up with a Plan B can weaken confidence and legitimize defeat. It was too bad that the law seemed to reinforce my worst traits. I ended up detached from the result, as if the diminished goal hadn't mattered that much in the first place.

Tibby had been staying close to her phone at a government agency a few blocks away. I ran through the latest events for her.

"Okay, now we've found Sarah Jones. We're about to disrupt her life in ways she's probably been dreading for forty years. What do you think, Tidbits?" I suppose I was trying to soften the moment—at least the anxiety I was feeling—by using one of the first nicknames I'd ever given her.

She answered without hesitation, with the confidence I lacked. "I don't think we should turn back now. We've had a long time to think about this." Tibby was convinced that my birth parents couldn't possibly *not* want to meet me. She had a romanticized image of my birth family waiting all those years for my triumphant appearance. They would all be standing at the front door of their fine house, shifting nervously on their feet, talking among themselves about what I would be like, craning to see our car turn into the driveway. Tibby could picture my waiting brother most clearly, that refined copy of me.

I sighed, trying to mask my excitement with cynicism. "You know, pal, this isn't one of your romance novels." Tibby reads faster than anyone I know. She races through thousands of pages a week, many of them mysteries and those mindless paperbacks with maidens being saved from despoilment in the final chapter.

I was sure that Tibby was scowling on the other end of the line. "No," she said, "but it isn't a Greek tragedy, either."

∗ ∗ ∗

"Do you think the hospital administrator idea will work? It seems kind of weak to me." I may have been talking about the believability of the story Kevin Holden's assistant was going to use in her call to my birth mother, but I was thinking about the shabbiness of deceiving my birth mother the very first time I was introduced to her.

Holden snorted into the phone. "Don't worry. Your mother will be so shocked by the call she won't be thinking all that clearly once she hears about you." Great. Now I get to shock a seventy-year-old lady.

I tried joking it off, for my benefit, not Holden's. "Doing it this way feels like I'm lying on a job application for a long-lost son. I'd hate to get fired after landing the job."

"Forget about it," Holden replied, sounding bored with the conversation. Deception was a regular part of his business.

Our assault on Sarah Jones began to produce consequences before I even knew the staged phone call had happened. My regular secretary was out on vacation, and the temp caught me in the lobby as I returned from a meeting across town. Anna looked like what she was: an old hippie, with stringy, graying hair down to her lower back. She had shown herself to be unfazed by anything I, or my overbearing partners, threw at her. Not this time. She must have been lurking near the elevator bank, guaranteeing that I wouldn't wander in the wrong direction on my return. If necessary, she was even going to head off a run to the men's room. When I caught sight of her hurrying toward me, I couldn't tell whether she was angry or about to cry or both.

"Anna! You okay? What's up?"

She spoke quickly, without much discernible space between her words: "There's a very abusive woman who's been trying to reach you. She's called three times and yelled at me when I told her you weren't here." Her tone suggested that I was to blame.

"Did she tell you her name?"

"Sarah Jones." We had been walking together toward my office. Now my shoes squeaked on the marble lobby floor as I spun toward Anna with a shocked look that she must have mistaken for anger. She reacted quickly, sounding as if she was begging for her life: "Please talk to her when she calls back. I can't take much more of this."

I had never heard anyone, other than Tibby or Holden, say my birth mother's name before. Suddenly she was no longer an abstraction. She was someone who had picked up the phone and called me, even if she might not be happy about it.

"Uh, okay," I stammered. "No problem." No problem? I had no idea what I was saying. "She seemed angry, huh?"

Anna looked like she was about to mimic my birth mother's anger, directed squarely at me, but she must have seen the confusion in my face. "Let's just say she doesn't seem too pleased with you, and I'm not likely to get a Christmas card from her either. Who the hell is she?"

I mumbled, "Just somebody I know," then ducked into my office and shut the door behind me.

I found a pink message slip from Holden on my desk, next to the three from Sarah Jones. Anna had drawn four thick exclamation points on the last one from my birth mother. I dialed Holden, fighting the light-headedness that hit me as I faced the unique experience of a confrontation with an angry woman I believed to be my biological mother. "What's happened, Kevin?" I demanded as soon as he picked up the phone. "Sarah Jones is apparently coming after me with a sledgehammer." I tried to lower the pitch of my voice and slow my words, but I sounded embarrassingly adolescent to myself.

"Yeah, listen." Holden was in rapid-fire mode, his voice strained. "I'm in a meeting but I'm trying to get my hands on the tape recording of the phone call between my investigator and Sarah. You should probably listen to it before you talk to her. She's denying she ever put up a kid for adoption."

"Not sure I can…" was all I got out before Holden cut me off.

"Sorry about this, but I gotta go." I expected to hear a dial tone, but he stopped short of hanging up. He hadn't expected my frustrated silence. "Look, David, there's no doubt she's your mother. Just sit tight for a few minutes. I'll get back to you as quick as I can." I agreed to wait for him before I returned Sarah's call, but hadn't reckoned on her persistence in trying to reach me.

Anna knocked on my door, pushed it open without waiting for an answer, and walked stiffly into my office. With the look and tone of a pouting toddler, she said, "It's her again."

I realized that it was time to get on with it, whatever "it" was going to be.

7

I picked up the phone, said a shaky "hello," and for the first time heard my birth mother's voice. It was cold and belligerent: "Who *are* you?" Her voice was strong, stronger than I would have expected from a woman her age.

"My name is David Ford, and I think you may be my mother." I knew she was my mother, but had to give her room. I forced myself to sound as much as I could like an announcer on a smooth-jazz radio station. I suppose that I was trying to soothe myself as much as Sarah Jones. My chest and shoulders tightened, adrenaline responding indiscriminately to a mix of fear and excitement.

"Well, I'm *not* your mother," she nearly shouted. "What do you want from me?" Her Virginia accent sounded like Mom's. It would have had a lilting quality if it hadn't been so hostile. She was nearly screaming into the phone.

"Mrs. Jones, I don't want anything from you. I must have made a mistake and I'm sorry to have bothered you." I shouldn't have interfered in the life of someone who wanted to be left alone. I didn't want to compound the agony by arguing with her. Or I may just have been bailing out, refusing again to face failure.

I listened to the silence. This would be the only conversation I ever had with my birth mother, and now it was over.

But Sarah Jones surprised me. She began to speak again, almost whispering into the phone. "I couldn't possibly be your mother." It sounded like she was trying to convince herself. Then she asked a question that I doubt many other children have heard from their mothers: "How would I know if you are my child?"

My birth mother wasn't ready to end the call. I resisted my instinct to be sarcastic, took a breath, and said evenly: "Mrs. Jones, if you had a baby boy on May 22, 1955, at the Medical College of Virginia in Richmond, and you gave the baby up for adoption, there's a *very* strong chance you are my mother." It was hard to find a gracious way to answer her question.

In that broad Virginia accent, the edge in her voice softening only a little, Sarah asked several more hostile and confused questions, all with the underlying premise that I was trying to harass or get something from her. Then, "Why are you picking on me?"

I shook my head, not knowing whether to be angry at the question or to feel sorry for her. "I'm not trying to pick on you, ma'am. I've had some health problems, and hoped you—I mean, my mother—might be able to help with my medical history." She said nothing.

I leaned back in my chair, worn down by the few minutes we had been on the phone, unsure how to set my birth mother free or to free myself from her. There didn't seem like much to be gained by stringing this out. "Mrs. Jones, I also wanted to let my mother know that I have a great life with a great family, and that everything has worked out well for me. If you are not my mother, then I apologize for bothering you. If you *are* my mother and this is your way of telling me to leave you alone, I promise you'll never hear from me again."

My birth mother said coldly, "Thank you very much," and hung up. The sudden rattle and click were hostile punctuation marks at the end of her final words. I looked around the room, reminding myself where I was, and caught the muffle of a noisy discussion in the hallway outside my closed door. What would the talkers think if they had heard the conversation I just had with my birth mother? Before calling Tibby, I sat for a few minutes trying to decide what *I* thought about the conversation. I wished Tibby could have been listening in on the line;

I didn't trust my powers of observation at a time like this, even if I felt that I could remember every word of the call.

The search for my brother had been shifted to Sarah, and now she had brought it all to an end. The Joneses wouldn't be waiting for Tibby and me at their front door for that joyful reunion. Could I just go straight after my brother? He was a forty-seven-year-old man at this point, free to make his own decisions, and it wouldn't take Holden long to find him now. But maybe meeting my brother, and the two sisters who hadn't even been part of my search, should wait until after Sarah Jones was long gone. That was beginning to feel like a good, safe answer. Yet another risk-averse Plan B.

* * *

I listened uneasily to the tape recording of the investigator lying to my birth mother about how I had contacted the hospital. I was an eavesdropper, abusing Sarah Jones's expectation of privacy once again.

Holden's assistant sounded innocent and chipper, not as if she were about to stun my birth mother: "Ma'am, I can assure you it's hospital policy not to give out the identity of birth mothers, but we try to get in touch with former patients when an inquiry is made. Your son doesn't know how to contact you."

Sarah Jones's tone was now familiar to me. "He's *not* my son! Why is he doing this to me?" She was panicked and angry.

"I don't know, Mrs. Jones." The investigator was trying to maintain her professional tone. "But our records show that you were admitted to our maternity ward and gave birth to a baby boy on the date this gentleman says he was born here."

"That's a lie," she insisted. "I have three children, and he's not one of them. You tell him to leave me alone. What does he want from me?"

The investigator was getting to experience the Sarah I had. "Ma'am,

I won't be speaking to him again, but if you'd like to, I can give you his address and phone numbers." That explained the calls to my office. I had stupidly expected to maintain control over future contacts. Lawyers like to attack and then run for cover, leaving as few traces as possible. Now I was as exposed as I had caused my birth mother to be.

Sarah Jones had been given more than my office phone number, a fact that I hadn't considered until Tibby called shortly before I headed home at the end of that long day. "You need to come home and listen to the answering machine." My wife's voice was calm but insistent. "She left a bunch of ugly messages here, screaming at you to return her calls." The "she" was obvious. Sarah Jones's hateful tone was old news to me, but this was Tibby's first direct exposure to her abuse.

"I'm sorry, little pal. Don't pay any attention to that crap." I wished I could have erased the messages before Tibby could hit the play button. She started to say something and then stopped. I kept on, in a softer tone, trying to show that I was past the hurt from Sarah Jones, even if it wasn't entirely true. "Pip. Forget about it. We're done with her." I hoped that we were done with Sarah Jones; she had rejected me and I wanted to rid her from my mind.

Tibby slowly said, "It's just that…why would she be so horrible?" Yes, my birth mother *had* been horrible. Tibby said what I didn't want to admit.

I scrambled to shove papers into my briefcase. I needed to go home to my wife. Her hopes for a storybook ending were gone, those answering-machine messages serving as the most tangible evidence.

* * *

I flew to Dallas early the next morning for a meeting that I couldn't avoid. I remember it only as foggy background noise to my stewing over the events of the day before. I rearranged my schedule to avoid an overnight stay, knowing that I would spend most of the day in airports or on airplanes.

I ducked my head down to stare out the porthole window on the return flight, watching the evening sky turn black. The hum of the plane's engines was comforting, a predictable stimulus for a change, but my mind wouldn't rest. I pulled the overpriced air-phone from its cradle in the seatback in front of me, something I rarely did, and called Tibby.

She would have been on her way to bed by then, not expecting to hear me come through the front door for hours. I expected a drowsy "hello," but she sounded as if she had been waiting for the phone to ring, an edgy impatience in her voice. "When I got home tonight, there was another message from Sarah on the machine."

I sagged into my seat as if pushed downward by turbulence, despite the smooth flight. "Sorry, Pip. More screaming?" I was trying to talk as quietly as I could over the hum of the cabin. My seatmate was snoring in my direction.

"The message is very strange. You'll need to listen to it when you get home to see if it makes any more sense to you than it does to me."

I thought that Tibby was just trying to protect me. "Come on, little guy. What did she say?"

"I'm serious. She seemed very confused, like she'd never spoken to you before."

I arrived home sometime after midnight. Tibby had waited up for me, far past her preferred bedtime. She groggily hugged me and left me in the den as I rewound the tape and heard Sarah Jones's cold voice once again. I listened to the message so many times that night that her words remain a crystal memory: "Why—and I'm going to put this very strongly—why have you not returned the call that you placed to me yesterday?" Sarah's belligerence filled the room. "My name is Sarah Jones. Now you better get back in touch with me or I'm going to get the police on you. You stop pestering me. You do something about it. Do you understand me?" Then, in a sarcastic, dark tone: "Bye, now." Her last words chilled me. Could my birth mother actually be evil?

She had asked if I understood her. No, I didn't understand at all, any better than Tibby had when she listened to the message. I thought that I had my first and final conversation with her the day before. Why was she calling again and acting as if we had never spoken? How was I to interpret her demand that I both call her back and stop pestering her?

Sarah Jones seemed unbalanced and irrational, even allowing for the shock my contact must have given her. This felt like just the beginning, something I wasn't going to be able to control. I flicked off the lights in the den, stopped in the doorway, then stepped back and sank into my desk chair. I had neglected to close the blinds on the windows when I came in, and now looked out at the maple tree whose web of bare limbs was brightly defined by the streetlight it had grown up around. Everything seemed so still, at peace, out there at that moment. Was there any point to going up to bed now? I doubted that the stillness would follow me to sleep.

* * *

I may have stuck my hand down the turtle hole once too often. Wes Sessoms and his old beagle had inadvertently taught me about that danger when we were teenagers kicking around the overgrown orange grove that surrounded his isolated house in the Florida countryside. We could hear the dog's muffled baying far off in the distance.

I was surprised. "How could Tye get so far away so fast?" I asked. "She was just here five minutes ago."

Wes laughed. "She ain't twenty feet from us." He pointed to a hole in the ground ahead of us: a gopher-turtle hole, like the ones we had plumbed for secrets as fearless kids, as easily home to rattlesnakes as to the turtle that may have dug it years before.

"No way," I said. "She's down in the hole?"

"It's her favorite thing, sniffin' out whatever's down there. We used to try to stop her, figurin' she'd end up tanglin' with a rattler or just get her ass stuck and never be seen again. But we gave up after a while."

"I didn't think those holes went much more than a few feet deep," I replied, smiling as Tye let out a long growl, this time sounding closer to the surface. Her tail suddenly appeared as she backed out of the hole. Her head emerged with big beagle ears flapping and the shell of a gopher turtle clamped in her teeth. The turtle had retracted its legs, head, and tail into the shell. Tye had a tight grip on the leading edge of the shell above the opening for the turtle's head. She yanked the turtle above ground and, with a shake of her head, sent the ten-pounder skittering along the sand. Chasing and pawing maniacally at her new toy, the dog flipped the turtle over and began to scratch at the flat underside of the shell.

Wes kicked loose dirt at the dog. "Tye, leave that stupid turtle alone," he yelled. "Go on, get away." The dog moved back, its soulful eyes looking up at Wes in disappointment. "Don't bother to look at me that way. You're lucky you don't have a rattler's fangs stuck in your nose."

My friend flipped the turtle over with the tip of his shoe and bent down to pick up the prehistoric-looking brown object with a hand under each side of the shell. I knew what he was going to do next; I had been the victim and perpetrator more than once. I jumped back as Wes spun around with the underside of the foot-long turtle aimed at me. I narrowly avoided the torrent of urine that flew from the terrified turtle in a volume that always surprised me when I saw it.

Wes laughed again, loudly. "Thought I had you that time." He dropped the turtle at the edge of its hole, then nudged it in with his shoe. The turtle was still for a few seconds, then seemed to understand where it was. Its head poked tentatively out of the shell, followed quickly by legs and tail, and the ugly brown shell dropped out of sight into the darkness of the hole. Tye barked angrily as Wes pulled her back by the collar, then launched her underhanded away from the turtle's retreat.

I stood over the turtle hole. It looked as dark and abandoned as the others I had first probed as a six-year-old. Big enough for a dog to get lost in, those holes obviously had more potential for trouble than I could have imagined.

Now, sitting in this dark room, churning through my brief history with Sarah Jones, trying to guess what might happen next, I wished I could go back and stop Kevin Holden's associate from making that first call to my birth mother. I doubted that I had seen all of this turtle hole's secrets, but was ready to leave the possibilities behind.

8

I returned my birth mother's call the next morning. Tibby listened in from her office and I felt her tension on the other end of the line. I wondered if she would remember to breathe as I dialed the number. I wondered if *I* would remember to breathe. An elderly man—I guessed my birth father—answered in a soft and shaky voice. "H – hello?"

"Hello. My name is David Ford and I'm returning Mrs. Jones's call to me yesterday." I tried to sound as neutral as I could. There would be plenty of time for stronger emotions if the call went in the wrong direction. I didn't allow myself to expect it to go in a good direction.

"Oh. My wife isn't feeling very well and may be asleep. I'll check." I could hear him wander off after letting the phone clatter to rest.

I whispered to Tibby, "You okay, Puddle-jumper?" I think I was trying to reassure myself as much as her. "Sounds like a fun guy, no?" Why not joke about someone who might be my father?

"*Callate*." "Be quiet" in Spanish, Tibby's second language. "He'll hear you."

Slow footsteps approached the phone. "I'm sorry. She *is* asleep. Could I have her call you back?"

"That's fine," I replied, as neutrally as I could. Great. Another delay in this nightmare. I gave him my phone number.

"Area code 2-0-2? Where's that?"

"Washington, D.C." Does he really not know who I am or what's going on? Would Sarah Jones not tell her husband about my dropping into their lives after four decades?

"Oh, I didn't know she knew anybody up there." He was good at this if it was an act.

I didn't know what to say next. Certainly not what I was thinking: "Just another one of your children." I played along as if I might have been calling about an AARP membership.

Dan Jones's tired voice filled the silence: "Well, I'll let her know you called. She might not call you back until tomorrow. Is that okay?"

"Sure," I said. "Just remind her I'm returning her call from yesterday. If she doesn't need to speak to me, she doesn't have to call back." I wanted the record to be clear that I wasn't breaking my promise never to be heard from again unless she approached me. My birth father seemed uninterested, as if he were just his wife's secretary.

After everything that would happen later, it's hard to accept this as the only contact I would ever have with my father. If I knew then what I know now, I might have seized the chance to engage Dan Jones. The way it turned out, though, my impressions of the man will always be filtered through the opinions of others.

* * *

Maybe it was perversely appropriate that the entirety of my relationship with my birth father was a brief telephone call. My life as a lawyer, and now as an adoptee looking for answers, was centered on the telephone, particularly before email became the communication method of choice. I had clients that I'd worked with for years, who had trusted me with problems that really mattered to them, but that I had never met in person. I had papered dozens of complicated transactions without even being in the same room with the lawyers on the other side.

I was no different from any of my law partners in my telephone habits, and I may have been more reasonable than some: A guy in the office next to mine was notorious for having all of his loud, profane calls projected down the hallway from his speakerphone. He never picked up the receiver to talk to anyone, regardless of the occasion. It was left to me one day to get up and pull his door shut as he listened to his teenaged daughter weep on the other end of the line about his acrimonious divorce from her mother. I had to dampen the sound of his cold, lawyer-precise answers to her sobbed questions.

I was only a telephone voice to the woman in the Virginia agency who might have knowingly failed to cut the name "Jones" out of my adoption records. I would never see Kevin Holden or his associate in person, despite their impact on my life. My voice was even more of an abstraction to my birth father, if he truly didn't know who I was when I called.

* * *

And now I was waiting for another call from Sarah Jones, which finally came through to my office the next day. My secretary was visibly relieved that I was there to take the call. She didn't know that I had spent the morning staring at the phone, waiting for this moment.

"Hello, Mrs. Jones. This is David Ford." It was my best attempt at a lawyer-as-formidable-opponent voice.

Sarah spoke haltingly, with none of the angry determination she had shown three days before. "My... my husband told me you called yesterday." Those few words were enough to hear a marked shift in tone, sad and subdued, almost as if she had just emerged from sleep. For that reason alone I was sorry I couldn't find a way to interrupt the call and secretly add Tibby to the line.

"Mrs. Jones, I hope he also told you I called only because you had left me a message asking me to." I realized that I still sounded stern, but I wanted her to understand that I wouldn't take more of her spite.

"I wasn't feeling very well yesterday," she explained haltingly. "I've been ill with diverticulitis and on Monday they gave me a new kind of shot for migraine headaches. I think the shot made me forget what happened over the last few days."

"Oh." Was she telling the truth or looking for an excuse for her behavior? I waited for her to speak again. I wanted to see where she was going.

"Who are you again? Are you a lawyer?" She sounded genuinely puzzled.

I wanted to say, "Are you kidding?" but controlled myself. I tried to put warmth into my voice. "Yes, ma'am, I am a lawyer. But as I told you the other day, I believe I'm your son."

"I thought you were a lawyer calling about my son."

I still had to resist the desire to respond sharply. I had been hurt more than I was willing to admit. I took a deep breath. "No. When we last spoke, I told you I thought I was your son and, if you wanted it that way, I'd never bother you again. I called again only because you left me another message at my home." Time to stop acting like a lawyer and more like a human being, I thought.

Sarah spoke as if she were talking to herself. "My husband—your father—has a bad heart and a defibrillator." I didn't know what a defibrillator was, but it sounded serious. "He put all this out of his mind a long time ago. I don't think he could bear it now." It hit me that she had said "your father." At least some of Kevin Holden's cynicism might not have been justified after all.

"I don't want to cause your family any trouble, Mrs. Jones. I'll leave it up to you to decide whether to have any further contact with me."

"My children don't know about you," she stated firmly. Her husband didn't want to know anything about me and her children didn't know anything about me. I was even more of an outsider to my birth family than I had imagined. My brother and sisters were slipping away from me.

She kept on: "Were your parents good people?" The question

surprised me. I tried to collect my thoughts, piecing together a rapid monologue about my wonderful and supportive parents, my education, and my marriage. At first I felt like I was writing my own obituary under deadline, three paragraphs, no photo. Then, whether for her benefit or mine, I volunteered the kinds of information that I guessed a birth mother would want to know from the child she had given up.

I was worried that the silence from her end of the line meant that Sarah Jones was not that interested. Maybe it was the medication she had mentioned that made her seem removed from the conversation, or maybe she was just terrified of finally talking to someone she had hoped never to hear from. I needed to guide her through this, much as you would a child in a new experience.

"I grew up in Florida, after my father graduated from the University of Virginia," I offered. "He went back to college after they adopted me, because he didn't want his son to grow up with a father who didn't have a degree." Silence. I kept going: "I went to my hometown college, where I met my wife. We got married after I graduated from law school. I went to U.Va. myself, partly because of Dad."

Still more silence from the other end of the line. I continued, "We don't have any kids." At least my birth mother was proving not to be the sort who was likely to ask me why that was. This call might really be the last one. I wanted it to end well, but I struggled with what to say next.

She perked up when I told her I was an only child. "That had been my instruction to the doctor and the lawyer who handled things," she recalled, almost dreamily. "I wanted you to be taken care of all by yourself." She didn't explain further. More space that I refused to fill, then: "When you were born, Dan's parents had a lot of medical problems. Boy, the nursing-home expenses were killing us."

I was hoping for more, but that seemed to be as much of an explanation as she was prepared to give. Smart negotiators always listen more than they talk; I fought the instinct to force the conversation.

Sarah finally filled the awkward void with a new topic. "I want you to know that we were married when you were born and we have been for forty-eight years." Translation: She wanted me to know that I wasn't a bastard, at least not literally.

Sensing that she was ready to end the conversation, I invited her to get in touch with me any time she wanted. She wrote down my home address and repeated back to me the phone numbers that she had abused just two days before.

"Mrs. Jones?" What was I supposed to call this woman? "If you'd like, my wife and I would be happy to come down and visit with you sometime."

Her answer was too quick, with none of the ambivalence I would like to have heard in her voice: "No, I think it's best to leave things alone. If Dan dies before I do, maybe things might be different. But not now." It sounded final, as if she had expected the question and was sure of the answer. My birth mother said goodbye wistfully—at least that's how I wanted to hear it—and hung up.

The call wasn't much longer than our first, but I felt the sweat of exhaustion under my shirt. I loosened my tie and stared at the bookshelf on the wall opposite my desk. It was lined with the thick, leather-bound volumes of all the big deals I had done over the years, the spines stamped in gold with the names of who bought what in one corporate acquisition after another. Clients loved to see their hard work (and my legal fees) memorialized so elegantly, and so did I. The books would never be the kinds of best sellers I would like to have written, even if I was paid good money for what they represented. They seemed to put messy deals into order, a tidy chronology of big chunks of my professional life. It was a fabrication to see the books that way; no transaction ever reduced itself so neatly to a few hundred pages between fancy covers. But that bookshelf momentarily represented a place in my life where questions could be answered with a lawyer's certainty.

∗ ∗ ∗

Tibby's disappointment softened, but was still tangible, as I described my conversation with Sarah. I'm not sure what I felt at the time. On the one hand, I had found my biological parents and thought I knew a little more about myself. On the other, I was no closer to my goal of meeting my brother and, now, my two sisters.

I wanted to be done with my birth family for a while and everyday demands gave me the excuse I needed to ignore them. I had complicated matters by deciding to shake myself loose from that oxygen-free law firm in favor of another. So, in the midst of my brush with Sarah Jones, I had been extricating myself from one place of employment while figuring out the bureaucracy at another. And no one but Tibby and my private investigator knew how far along we had taken the search for my birth family; I was too skittish to tell even my adoptive parents what I had been up to.

I moved forward in isolation, projecting normalcy to friends and co-workers. That seemed better for now: fewer people expecting the latest news, especially at a time when I wasn't sure what I thought about what was happening. I wanted perfection and what I saw as the symmetry of completeness, an emotional framework that left me no room to appreciate how far I had traveled in just the last four days.

I could pick up the chase for my brother and sisters another day. Going back to being the only child was beginning to feel like a welcome retreat, but I needed Tibby to feel good about how things had ended, too. We were standing in the kitchen that night after opening a bottle of wine. She wasn't buying my enthusiasm for taking a vacation from my birth family. I pushed the issue: "Come on, Pip, aren't you kinda glad it's over with?"

She had put down her glass and was working through the day's junk mail. Now she leaned toward me and shook her head. "It's not over." Tibby was frowning, reacting to the defeatism underlying my latest philosophy. Her frown turned to a puzzled look as I smiled at her. She was my greatest asset, quick to remind me of my strengths, tolerant of my weaknesses, and a sharp-eyed critic of those who weren't. She would protect me, whether I deserved it or not.

9

O n Mothers Day, 1995, I was studying the *Washington Post* while Tibby skimmed the *New York Times*. It was a bright spring morning, not yet warm enough to draw us onto the flagstone patio visible through the French doors. Our open kitchen looked out over the family room a few steps below; Tibby sat on a tall stool at the counter, looking like a captain on the bridge of her ship. She plowed through the thick Sunday editions in the time it took to drink her second, oversized mug of coffee. I never would have been a speed-reader, even without my lawyer-lust for details, but I could easily get lost in an article that interested me.

I was laid out on a sofa at the far end of the room, with the stereo turned up, as usual a little louder than Tibby would have liked. I yelled over the music: "Here's another one of those Mothers Day stories about a woman who gave up her baby for adoption and has been pining away ever since wondering what became of her child." My tone was sarcastic. Sarah hadn't been heard from since the call nearly three months before. "So do you think I should give 'Mommy Dearest' a call?"

Tibby knew I didn't mean Mom. We had both already completed the greeting-card-and-phone-call ritual with our mothers. She refused to play along. "No, she would faint." Silence for a few beats. "But I still don't think you've heard the last from her."

I jumped up, walked over to the stereo, and turned down the volume. "Come on. That last call was pretty final. Besides, if she sticks with the pattern, I'm afraid her next call would be one of those shrieking things, where she threatens to have me incinerated if I don't give her back her genetic material." I couldn't admit my disappointment that Sarah hadn't called again; I had held out a slight hope that time would lessen the shock of my sudden appearance in her life. Maybe she would have talked to her husband about me after all; maybe his heart wouldn't have exploded (or whatever defibrillators are supposed to prevent) and he would have encouraged some sort of contact with his family.

Tibby had plenty of experience with me in full self-protective mode. Flipping to the next page of the paper without looking up, she said: "Wait and see." She wasn't going to debate with me.

* * *

Tibby dropped me off at the end of our driveway after we had run errands that afternoon. She was going grocery shopping without me. I had used one of my standard lines: "Gee, I'd love to go, too, but I've got to get some things done for tomorrow morning's meeting." This time she knew that I probably would prefer to go grocery shopping rather than sit in the house on a nice Sunday afternoon drafting yet another boring legal document.

The answering machine was beeping as I came through the front door. I punched the button and heard a woman's formal voice, one I didn't recognize. "This is Linda Farmer from Columbus, Ohio. I have a confidential matter to discuss with David Ford regarding Sarah Jones." I hadn't expected to hear that name from a stranger any time soon. Linda Farmer, whoever she was, had my attention. She continued in a hard tone as she gave me her phone numbers and asked me to call her back as soon as possible.

Few people in my universe knew the name Sarah Jones, or that I had any connection to her. If I had been quiet about my adoptive past before finding my birth parents, I became statue-silent on the topic after the emotions Sarah had put us through. I should have told my parents about finding Sarah, but I couldn't pull them into something so discouraging. And I was still trying to rationalize why I would have been the only one of the Jones's four children put up for adoption.

I knew that both of my birth sisters lived in Virginia, not Ohio, so it couldn't be one of them. I couldn't resist lawyering the situation: Maybe this Linda Farmer person was some sort of advocate for birth parents calling to tell me to lay off. But why would that be necessary, when I backed out of Sarah Jones's life as soon as I had entered it?

There was only one way to find out. I picked up the phone, started to dial, looked at the keypad for a few seconds, and hung up. I grabbed a pen and dug into my briefcase for a writing pad. I looked out the window at my neighbor washing his car. Maybe I should wash my car, wait for Tibby to get home. I sighed, then picked up the phone again.

"Hello?" It was the same voice I had heard on the answering machine.

"This is David Ford calling for Linda Farmer." I tried to copy her serious tone.

"This is Linda, David." Pause. "Do you know who I am?"

"No."

"Do you know who Sarah Jones is?"

"Yes."

"Do you know that you have a brother and two sisters?"

"Yes." It was beginning to feel like the twenty-questions game, but I checked myself from rudely asking what this was all about.

Linda paused; I decided to wait her out. She began but failed to complete a couple of sentences, then said: "Are you strong? I have quite a story to tell you."

I started to say, "Yeah, I work out a little," but decided that this wasn't the time for a weak joke. "Okay. I'm all ears." It was dawning on me that this was going to be a different conversation than what I had feared.

"I'm your sister, too." It was a small sentence with a big impact, but I'm not sure I understood the words at first. How could she be my sister, too? She wasn't one of the three siblings I had just gotten used to knowing about. My mind was not ready for whatever this woman was trying to tell me.

As unprepared as I'd been a few months before, when the private investigator had made another simple declaration about the two younger sisters I didn't know I had, this woman's plain statement of fact left me rudderless. I had come to terms with being one of four siblings, even if I was the only one put up for adoption. Now what was going on?

Linda spoke evenly, without any of the emotion she must have been feeling. "After they had their first son, Sarah and Dan Jones gave up three girls and a boy for adoption. I was the third and you were the last. The three of us girls all made contact with Sarah over the years and eventually learned about each other. We found each other twelve years ago and have been looking for you ever since. Now we've found you!" Linda's voice cracked; I thought she might be crying. The solemn voice was gone.

I still can't relive the moment without it inducing the same emotions, a chemical euphoria, that I felt at the time. Describing the next few hours seems like trivializing them. How do I do justice to events that would forcibly redefine my life and the lives of those closest to me?

I wish that I had hit "record" on the answering machine that afternoon. My taped voice would have quickly shifted in tone from lawyer to adolescent. I would have been grabbing at Linda's words, struggling to fit them into my reality. I was once again dependent on the telephone, listening to a disembodied voice on the other end as it inserted me into a new family.

Linda was waiting for me to say something. She had to be worried about how I would respond to her. Instead of signaling the emotions that I was feeling, I instinctively retreated into the comfortable role of lawyer as information gatherer: "Looking for me? How were you looking for me?" What difference did it make? Three unknown sisters had been trying to find me. I liked the idea, even if I was acting like the slow kid in the back of the classroom. Maybe having three older sisters would have been even better than a brother back when I was trying to fit in with my schoolmates.

Linda sounded impatient. "We had all gotten good at searching for our birth parents, so we knew the adoption-search community pretty well," she explained. "We put entries in all the directories, all the usual stuff. But you would have had to be looking for us. Now that doesn't matter." She wasn't interested in that part of the story, and it wouldn't mean that much to me, but I had fallen into it while my emotions struggled to catch up.

Our formless conversation wandered through lives we hadn't shared, who was married to whom, how many nieces and nephews I suddenly had through my three new sisters (ten), what everyone did for a living, all of the obvious milestones. I grabbed a legal pad and wrote wildly as Linda's voice filled my ear with the compressed details of a half-century of lives lived. This was the last time that I could shamelessly ask about details like birth dates and kids' names that in a "normal" family would be scandalous not to remember.

One of Linda's first questions to me was: "What do you look like?"

"I'm six-four, kinda skinny, black hair, brown eyes."

"Darn."

"What's wrong with that?" I didn't think my description sounded that bad.

"You look just like the rest of them. I'm a redhead, with pale blue eyes and fair skin. I guess I'm destined to be the only one who got her looks from Sarah's side of the family."

I smiled at the idea that I looked like the rest of them. Was it likely that all seven of us would be the product of one set of parents? Kevin Holden would have said "no." I had spent the last two months thinking I was the only one out of four children given up for adoption. I hadn't wanted to find out that I was the result of one of the evil acts on the investigator's list, and that I had been rejected for it.

Now I could begin to relax, to dismiss my doubts, even if I still didn't understand my place in the story. "So, Linda, did you ever think that maybe you're not a purebred like the rest of us?" I asked, finally letting my irreverence seep into the conversation. "Maybe you're just a half-sister."

"Cut that out!" she groaned in mock protest. Then in a more serious tone, she confessed that the thought had crossed her mind, too. "Of course, me and my smart mouth, I once told Sarah I was sure I was the milkman's daughter. She didn't think that was so funny. But I *do* have the same build as everybody else." Her laughter came easily, starting low in the throat and ending in a high giggle. "Just like Sarah, you couldn't tell I was pregnant until I was about to drop."

I was so focused on our conversation that I didn't hear Tibby push through the back door, her arms loaded with grocery bags. She saw me on the telephone through the glass panels of the door into my office, my head down as I listened intently, and got on with dinner preparations.

Long into the call I realized that Tibby had no idea of the event that was unfolding. I pulled open the door and twisted around the corner, waving broadly to get her attention. She turned toward me, puzzled when she saw that I was still on the phone. I signaled for her to come over to my office and held up my legal pad to show her the scrawl: "I'm talking to one of my sisters!!" I was in the mood for double exclamation points, a rarity for me.

Tibby's frown changed to wide-eyed surprise. I nodded with a grin that said it was a good thing, not a variation on the calls with Sarah Jones. She went back to acting busy in the kitchen, trying to listen in on my side of the conversation and guessing about which of my two birth sisters might be on the phone.

I wanted to yell to her that I was no longer an only child. I hadn't felt like I had a brother and two sisters after my encounters with Sarah. No matter what else happened, now I had three sisters who had spent years trying to be my sisters.

Tibby would ask a lot of questions. I interrupted Linda. "Let me get this straight. Dawn is only a year younger than Greg, so that makes her six years older than me?"

"Right."

"Then Noelle was born thirteen months later?"

"Uh huh."

"Then you, fifteen months after that."

Linda laughed again. "Sarah and Dan were busy, weren't they? She told me all Dan had to do was look at her and she got pregnant."

"Took a couple of years off before having me, though." Sarcasm crept into my voice.

"Thank the Korean War and Dan's time in the Army Reserves for that. But they still managed to have four kids in seven years that they gave away. How could they have stayed sane?"

It was my turn to laugh. "Based on my two conversations with Sarah, I'm not so sure she did."

10

L inda spoke faster, as if making up for lost time. "Dawn and Noelle were delivered by the same obstetrician. He arranged to have them placed with the same family—without Sarah and Dan finding out at the time. So they got to grow up together, knowing they were real sisters."

She made a little noise, a derisive snort. "Sarah still gets angry about how that doctor betrayed her. I guess she thought he had agreed to get both babies adopted into families where they'd be only children. Who knows?"

It sounded to me like Linda had an ongoing relationship with Sarah, something I couldn't imagine. She kept on: "If Sarah and Dan hadn't moved to California by the time they had me, I bet the *three* of us would have been raised together. You know, I've also wondered whether they moved to California to cover their tracks. I think they went there because of his Army service, but you never know with those two."

Linda was the second child adopted by her parents, who later gave birth to two boys the doctors thought they couldn't have. She had led a military childhood, her family following the father from one Navy base to the next. That explained her neutral accent, just like mine. We would be the only two of the Jones's seven children without some variety of a Southern accent.

Linda quickly described Dawn and Noelle's enthusiastic parents and their modest lifestyle. The four of us had come from the same place, in a sense, and had ended up in very different families. But what emerged from Linda's words, even at this early stage, was that we had the common experience of being loved by the parents who had adopted us. I was beginning to think that my three new sisters and I were lucky to have been pushed away by our birth parents, at least after the narrow exposure I'd had to Sarah.

My sister knew a lot about this scattered collection of people. "How did you learn all of this?" I asked. "Sarah didn't tell me anything that would have led me to you."

"Just like you, we all found Sarah on our own," Linda explained. "I guess when we hit child-bearing age, we wanted to know what genes we were passing along. After the first bad contacts with her, I tried to stay in touch, calling her once or twice a year. One day she surprised me by telling me about the three of you—just that you existed, nothing more. After that, I made it my mission to drag out of her what I needed to know so I could find you."

She came out with a guilty little laugh. "To be honest, I'm not sure I would have stayed in touch as much as I did if I hadn't thought I could get what I wanted out of her. A lot of those calls were hard. She can be so emotional, wanting you to feel sorry for her one minute and then threatening never to talk to you again."

The emotional extremes sounded familiar. "I got a little of that myself," I said with a touch of acid in my voice. "Actually more than enough of it." Maybe it was good that I only had two doses of Sarah Jones.

Linda wanted to keep the story going, as if I hadn't interrupted. "Anyway, Sarah told me that Dawn and Noelle were delivered by the same doctor, whose name she claimed not to remember at first. A while later, she said two of her obstetricians had the same name, but she couldn't remember which babies they delivered. *Finally*, and I mean maybe a year after I started talking to her, she told me that Dawn, Noelle, and one of the other kids—but she claimed she couldn't remember which one—had all been delivered by doctors named Morrison. I knew my obstetrician's name wasn't Morrison, so I decided to go with the idea that it had to be you guys, not one of the two girls she had after us."

"Weird," I responded. "Had Sarah gone looking for Dr. Morrisons in the yellow pages?" Linda mostly referred to our birth mother by her first name, so I hesitantly adopted the same informality for an old woman I didn't really know. "Kind of like those serial murderers who always leave the same clues?"

Linda laughed again, this time one of her deep barks. "You got me," she said. "I think it was just coincidence, but with Sarah you can't tell. She's complicated. Maybe she did it just to confuse things more than they already were."

Linda admitted, again with a laugh, to being confused about which doctor did what, who was born when and where. Once Sarah began to open up to her, Linda had simply written everything down to study later, just as I was doing at that very moment. There was a sudden urgency in Linda's voice. "I didn't dare to interrupt her once I got her talking. I was afraid that anything I said might cause her to shut up forever."

I was glad to hear that Linda had been confused. She was giving me the condensed version, and I was starting to lose track myself. Still trying to keep up with every word my new sister spoke, I looked down at my notepad for reassurance: "Dawn—first kid given up for adoption—then Noelle—same family adopted her—then Linda—born in California." Then me.

Linda wasn't waiting for my confusion to clear. "So I went nuts. I knew approximately when the three of you were born, but Sarah was fuzzy even on that, so I started looking for the doctors. I just decided to follow the hunch that Sarah was giving me a clue—but not willing to tell me clearly, or maybe she wasn't clear on the facts anymore herself—that you were the other one delivered by a Dr. Morrison. She made me work for every little bit of information. I could never get whether she was purposely manipulating me, didn't really remember anymore, or was too psychologically fragile to talk about it."

Whatever else I was learning about my birth family, I was discovering that I liked my new sister Linda. She was smart, thoughtful, and showed a sense of humor where others, including me, might have given up in frustration. In fact, I *had* given up in frustration, or at least pessimistic resignation.

She shifted into a story-telling monologue, taking herself, as much as me, back to her own struggle years before. "It wasn't all that hard to find the two doctors, but neither was very cooperative at first. Actually, your Dr. Morrison gave me no real help at all. He stuck with patient confidentiality as his excuse. But Dawn and Noelle's doctor didn't completely shut me out."

Linda paused, remembering the moment, then spoke with the strong voice she must have used with the doctor back then. "Once he heard all the stuff that I already knew—Sarah and Dan's names, what Sarah had told me about him delivering two of their daughters—I think he realized I wasn't going to stop until I got what I wanted, and he softened. Just wait. You'll see what I'm like when I want something. He told me he needed a couple of days to think about it and would call me back."

"When was this?" I asked.

"1983. I know the year because I just looked it up—almost exactly twelve years ago. I can't believe it's taken this long to find you."

I laughed. "It's genetic. I inherited our birth parents' ability to hide in the open." Back to my new reality: "How long did the doctor make you wait?"

"Three painful days. Actually, two of them were over the weekend, but the waiting nearly killed me. A bunch of my co-workers had known for years about my efforts to find my birth parents, and then our sisters, and—finally—you, so they were asking questions all the time. So were our friends."

I interrupted. "I had taken the opposite approach, not telling anyone anything."

"Not my style," Linda laughed. "My husband tried not to ask too many questions, but he was living every minute of it, too. They all meant well, but it made the waiting at every step even worse."

Linda's cadence quickened, as if she wanted to get on to the happy ending. "When Dr. Morrison eventually called me back, I could tell he was still pretty uncomfortable with telling me anything and I was afraid he was going to get away. So I told him I didn't need to contact Dawn and Noelle directly. He could pass on to their parents that you and I existed, and that I would love to be a part of their lives if they were interested. I really didn't want to turn their lives upside-down."

"Did you seriously worry that...," I began, looking down at my notes to make sure I had the names right, "...that Dawn and Noelle wouldn't want to meet you?" I couldn't imagine any of my new sisters not wanting to be a part of this.

"Not really, but you never know," she said. "Sarah told me that Dawn and Noelle had tried to make contact with her, so they must have been open to something." But Linda wasn't so sure how the two older girls' parents would feel about sudden contact with their birth family: "One thing I learned through years of working with other adoptees is that adoptive parents can be pretty protective of their relationships with their kids."

I nodded. For all of my mother's support, I still wasn't sure that my parents would be fine with all of this, either.

Linda kept to her fast-paced monologue. "I didn't know whether Dr. Morrison was trying to protect the Dicksons—the girls' adoptive family—or just trying to preserve the doctor-patient thing. Thank

God he finally said okay. He told me he was still sorry that Sarah and Dan moved to California when she was pregnant with me. Sounds like I really might have grown up with my sisters if he had delivered me. He did seem upset that he couldn't keep us together."

"Interesting. Of course, if we're playing the 'what-if' game, I guess if they had stayed in one place the whole time they were dropping us off on doorsteps, all four of us might have been raised together. But, then, maybe the Dicksons would have raised the white flag after the first two and said, 'Enough!'"

"Could you imagine?" Linda laughed. "Then I would have been able to torture you."

"And I would have been able to annoy your boyfriends, the way little brothers are supposed to."

"I would have locked you in a closet," Linda announced, laughing once again. She was quick to laugh.

Linda returned again to speculating about our mother. "I really think Sarah and Dan might have moved around the way they did to make sure nobody figured out what they were doing." She was guessing, of course, trying to understand motives that would never have been her own. "It's amazing. No one in their families, not even their parents, ever found out about us, not to this day. I'm sure the welfare agencies never put it all together. If they had, don't you think they would have tried to step in and do something?"

How could our birth parents have hidden all of those unwanted births so effectively? Linda tried to answer her own question. "At least you'd think the state would get pretty nosy about it. Four kids in a row does seem to suggest instability, to put it mildly."

I thought back to events of only a few months before. "Judging from the way Sarah treated me, I'd say she wouldn't have been very pleased to get a visit from a county social worker asking about *four* unwanted babies."

"She would have gone berserk," Linda enthusiastically agreed. "No telling what Dan would have done, but she would have gone into a total panic. They probably would have disappeared in the night to protect Sarah's image of their reputation. Wait until you hear her talk about her illustrious family heritage."

I interrupted. "Not very likely. I'm not sure I need to have more conversations with her."

"You never know. I developed a relationship with her. An odd one, I admit. And you have to give her credit for letting us know the others were out there."

I still wasn't feeling very generous toward my birth mother. "Maybe, but she hadn't gotten around to telling *me* anything about you three. And it wasn't in me to try to stay in touch with her like you did. So you'll have to give me time to warm up to the concept."

I shook my head, silently agreeing with myself. "Sorry. I interrupted you. What about this family heritage thing?"

"I could never decide whether Sarah was more interested in hiding the craziness from her family—for the obvious reasons, I guess—or from the rest of the world because of the damage she thought it would do to the glorious family name. You know, the Wise family, the governor of Virginia, that stuff. You know what I'm talking about?"

"I heard a little from my mom, and then later when I saw my adoption lawyer's records," I said, nodding to myself. "I guess the Joneses made a big deal out of it when they had their interview with him."

Linda's laugh took on a caustic tone. "I'm not surprised; it means a lot to her. I tried to convince her that no one would care if it all came out in the open, that no one was interested in that sort of stuff anymore, but she wasn't going for it."

"So what happened when the doctor finally put you in touch with Dawn and Noelle's family?" I asked, pleased with myself for calling them by their right names without looking at my notes.

"Mildred Dickson, their mother, was great," Linda said brightly. "She called me right away, asked me a million questions. I'm sure some of them were just out of curiosity, but I think she also wanted to decide whether I was a nut case before she exposed her daughters to me."

"I'm still not sure you *aren't* a nut case," I laughed. She was already easy to joke with, as if we actually had grown up together. "What did *she* decide?"

Linda bark-laughed again. "I think she decided like everybody else: I'm a nut case, but harmless. We eventually met, we cried, the whole Hallmark-Hall-of-Fame moment. I don't want to diminish it. It was fantastic. But we can talk about all that later."

That was okay with me. I was feeling overwhelmed. And I had my own questions. "So what about me? What took you so long to find me? Just not interested? Some kind of girls-versus-boys thing?" I had faked a hurt tone of voice.

"Give me a break. I really worked at it, then Dawn and Noelle joined in. We tried the informal adoption search network. We advertised for a boy born on your birthday, or what we thought was your birthday. May 22, 1955, right? It was hopeless with the skimpy details Sarah gave me. To be fair, I guess she didn't really know much more about you than your birth date and where you were delivered—and maybe the name of your doctor. Always dead ends."

"But you kept on talking to Sarah over the years, hoping for more details?" I asked.

That was the part I still couldn't grasp, my birth mother's hostility still too recent a memory. Should I have tried harder with Sarah after she finally calmed down, even if I wouldn't have known the right questions to ask? It wouldn't have occurred to me to ask my birth mother whether she had others like me out there. Sarah might have broken if I had asked her why I was the only one of four given up for adoption, but I hadn't been brave enough to try. Linda's maternal instincts, the need to find things out for her unborn children, were stronger than my instincts to back away.

"Yeah," she sighed. "Like I said, maybe she was holding back, maybe she just couldn't remember anymore. Maybe there wasn't anything more to remember. I even visited her in her home once. I took Matt to see her when he was a newborn." I reviewed my notes quickly. Matt was Linda's oldest child, age thirteen.

"*That* was strange," Linda admitted. "Sarah kept insisting that I meet her husband but said I'd have to pretend to be someone else, just a friend. She had told me before that he put all of us out of his mind and wouldn't be able to handle the strain of meeting me. I told her that I didn't want to meet him under false pretenses, but she suddenly called out to him in the other room. I didn't even know he was at home. He came in, I stammered a 'hello,' and then he went back to his room. I was really upset with Sarah for manipulating me that way, so I left fairly quickly after that."

Linda had actually seen both of our birth parents. "What do good ole Mom and Dad look like?" I asked the question casually, but I was desperate to see something of myself in these peoples' faces, if only to confirm in some small way that I was really from them. I needed a little tangible proof.

"I'll send you the few pictures I've managed to get from Sarah over the years," Linda promised. "Dan was a fairly good-looking guy when he was younger, but the years have been rough on him. I think he's been a heavy smoker and drinker. Most of us got our build and coloring—yeah, except mine—from Dan, but we have Sarah's nose. Sounds kinda funny: 'getting somebody's nose.' Sarah, you'll have to see for yourself. She wasn't bad looking, but not the greatest beauty. Actually, the years haven't been too kind to her, either."

"How many times have you seen them?"

"I've only seen Dan in person the one time," she said. "But I guess

I've visited with Sarah three times now. Most of my contact has been over the phone, with cards and letters once in a while. Yeah," she admitted cynically, "that's right, staying in touch because I wanted to make sure I got everything out of her I could to help us find you."

"Tough job," I said with admiration.

"Maybe. But I also felt sorry for Sarah. Sometimes it seemed like I was the only person she had to talk to," Linda said softly. "I could tell she didn't have a close relationship with her kids. Her relationship with her husband was complicated. I guess I decided she'd given birth to me and needed a friend, so I would try to help her."

Linda had a generosity that I was afraid I lacked.

11

The late afternoon sun drifted into my eyes. I squinted, reached across my desk to close the slats of the plantation shutters, and realized that my home office, a tight space, had gotten mid-May warm while I talked with Linda. My right ear felt stuck to the telephone, so I loosened my grip on the handset and stretched to grab the doorknob to my left, immediately feeling the spread of cooler air that followed the door's swing into the room. I could hear a pan lid rattling softly on the stove at the other side of the house, but I wasn't close enough to smell what was cooking. An acorn fell through the top grill of the big air conditioner outside my window, twanging repeatedly against the spinning blades until it finally dropped like a ball through the flapping paddles of a pinball machine.

I leaned back in my chair, straightening from the slouch my mother warned would become a hunchback. A lot had changed in the last hour, but most things hadn't.

My focus returned to my newfound sister. "Did Sarah tell you about me today?" I asked.

"Yes. I try to call her on her birthday, sometimes on my birthday, and I called this afternoon to wish her a happy Mothers Day, because I wasn't sure her children would. I hate to say this, but she's devious. In the middle of our conversation she says to me, 'Oh, I talked to your brother a while ago.' I was sort of like, 'That's nice,' but I didn't really focus on it. I thought she was just telling me that her son Greg had checked in. So I said, 'How is Greg doing?' and she said, 'No, the other one.'"

I jumped in. "Like, 'Oh, by the way?'" I couldn't decide whether the idea was sickening or perversely funny.

"Uh huh," she said. "I froze. I knew from years of talking to her that if I just said, 'What?! Where is he?', she would clam up and it would take a long time, maybe forever, to get it out of her. So I tried my best to act casual about it, all the while my heart's racing. I was *this* close to finding you. I wasn't going to let you slip away. I asked her what had happened, but didn't push for how to find you. She's still convinced we're going to spill her secret and your arrival would make her even more paranoid.

"We kept chatting away and eventually she told me your name and mentioned that you gave her your address and phone number. I got up the nerve to ask her if she had them handy. She claimed she wasn't sure where they were, but guessed she could look for them. I said, 'I'll wait while you look,' and held my breath. When she said 'okay' and put the phone down, I listened to her digging around and prayed that she wouldn't come back on the line with an excuse. But, bless her heart, she gave me your home phone number and then I had to pretend to be interested in the rest of our conversation. I was desperate to get off the phone and call you."

Years of effort had come to an end with the call. I had been my sisters' long-term project without any idea that they existed.

Sarah Jones had told me that her children didn't know about us. It was time to sort that out. "What about her kids?" I grinned to myself. "I mean the three she kept."

"Sarah and her son Greg—they have a difficult relationship," Linda explained. "She doesn't like either of his two former wives and thinks he isn't as successful as he should be. I get the sense he's the black sheep. He has a kid from each of his marriages, but I don't know much about them."

I thought about the storybook image Tibby had always had of my older, wiser brother. It was beginning to sound like he might not be what she was hoping for.

I was back to scribbling as quickly as I could. Now it was the details of the kids my birth parents kept that I needed to record. "You haven't met any of the three, um, Keepers, have you?" I asked.

"Keepers?" Linda sounded puzzled.

"Yeah, as opposed to us Throwaways?" I instantly liked the irreverence of the labels.

She didn't seem impressed with my sour joke. "Sarah doesn't want us anywhere near them. Let's see what else I can tell you."

My handwriting got sloppier as I filled another page and flipped to the next. Linda had moved on to Mary, the sister born fifteen months after me, the sibling who immediately seemed the hardest for me to understand. What had changed in the lives of my birth parents in the space of those fifteen months? Why give up a fourth child in a row, then resolve to keep the next?

Linda wasn't going to let me wander far from her main story line. "Mary was in the military and her husband's an Army major. I think they live somewhere south of Washington, maybe not too far from you." I smiled to myself at the idea of having a sister so close by.

Even though Mary lived farther away from Sarah than the other two, Linda had the sense that she stayed in closer touch with her mother. "But there's some kind of heavy mother-daughter tension between the two that I've never had the will to get into with Sarah," Linda said, almost dismissively.

I broke in, trying to keep up with my new sister. "Sounds to me like you've psychoanalyzed Sarah pretty heavily for years. You haven't got that angle covered, too?"

"You're making me feel guilty." She put on a pathetic tone. "All I've tried to do is help our birth mother feel better about herself—and, by the way, find you."

I replied in a pseudo-German accent. "Sorry, sorry, Doctor Freud. Please continue."

"Jerk. Is it too early to call you that? And stop interrupting," she barked. "Okay. Ellie, actually it's Charlotte Ellen, is the youngest."

I interrupted, despite my sister's warning. "I assume that Ellie was another quick pregnancy. Seems like everybody, other than me, was born something like thirteen or fifteen months apart."

"Nope. Not this time. More like six years. Sarah said Ellie was a real surprise." It struck me that, with the family-planning skills my birth parents seemed to lack, it would be hard to single out any one of their children, whether given up for adoption or not, as more of a surprise than another.

Linda seemed to know the least about Ellie. "I think she's an artsy type, an art historian or something like that. Works for a museum. By the way, all three kids graduated from good colleges, so Sarah and Dan must have done something right along the way."

I had gotten to the bottom of what seemed like a long list of names—my family, but not my family. I would commit those names to memory later on. I had more important things to understand at the moment. "Do the three kids—the Jones kids, that is—know about us?"

"I know at least one of them does, but I'm not sure about the others. Mary, the one born just after you, has to know at least some of the story because Dawn confronted her when Mary was a teenager." I still had to prompt myself that Dawn was the oldest girl and the first of us given up for adoption. "Actually I think an intermediary confronted her for Dawn."

"What happened?" I asked.

"I guess Dawn and Noelle tracked down Sarah and Dan and tried to make contact."

"When would this have been?"

"Dawn and Noelle would have been in their early twenties, so sometime in the early '70s," Linda guessed. "It might have been around the time Dawn got married and became a Mormon. At some point she started doing the genealogy research that's important to the church."

Dawn and Noelle eventually got up the nerve to send a registered letter to the Joneses. "Sarah called one or both of them and gave them pretty much the same treatment as the first time you and I called her," Linda said.

"Dawn took it pretty hard, but Noelle eventually tried to smooth things over with Sarah, like I did. They were so young and Sarah's violent reaction broke their hearts. Can you imagine? Sarah had been afraid of that moment for twenty years, and suddenly these naïve girls show up looking for something Sarah wasn't going to give them."

I skimmed my own memories. "I didn't know how to deal with it when I got the treatment at thirty-nine," I admitted. "They found her before you did?"

"A few years before me," Linda said. "I guess they had each other to egg on. You know it took courage."

I did know. "What did they do next?"

"I've never really pushed the girls about it but, according to Sarah, Dawn and her husband eventually used a church mediator to make direct contact with Mary. I'm not exactly sure why Mary. I guess she did what anybody would do when someone came up to her on the sidewalk and said: 'You have sisters you don't know about who want to meet you.' It was Sarah's worst nightmare."

"How'd that end up?" I asked.

"Not so good. I guess Mary ran away, denying she knew anything about them. Sarah says it really traumatized her. But I get the sense that Sarah was less worried about Mary's feelings than that the cat was out of the bag. Whatever happened, it seemed to bring Dawn down to earth and they never tried anything like that again. I think Noelle somehow developed an on-again-off-again relationship with Sarah, sort of like mine. You know, phone calls every once in a while, a letter sometimes. That is, letters *to* Sarah, not *from* her. Sarah never wrote to us, at least never to me for sure."

Probably didn't want to leave any fingerprints, I thought. "What does Sarah have to say about all this?"

"She goes silent if I mention Dawn's name. I've tried over and over to see if I could get Sarah to talk with her, but it's no use. Besides, Dawn is very hurt herself and might not participate even if Sarah was willing."

"What about Dan? Where's he in all of this?" In the time we had been talking, Linda scarcely mentioned our birth father.

"His head's in the sand." Her tone was bitter. "He denies we ever existed."

"Does he know we've reappeared over the years?"

"He knows I've been talking to Sarah. He's even answered the phone a few times when I called. It's really weird. I'm pretty sure he knows who I am, but I just tell him I'm Sarah's friend Linda. He says 'hang on a minute' and puts the phone down. Whenever she mentions us, he acts like he doesn't know what she's talking about and leaves the room. Or at least that's what she says."

"You don't believe her?"

"I take an awful lot of what she says with a grain of salt," Linda acknowledged. "It's really hard to tell what she's up to when she tells you something. I'm sorry to make her sound bad, but that's the way it is."

I thought I already understood that part of my mother's personality. "No problem with me," I assured her. "You have a much more positive view of her than I do."

I wanted more information about my birth father. "Sarah told me he had a serious heart condition and wouldn't be able to bear the strain."

Linda sighed, as if in resignation. "I guess the heart condition is real, but his attitude has been constant over the years I've known Sarah. She's more at peace these days letting the heart thing excuse his inability to own up to the past." Linda had lived with this a lot longer than I had.

My new sister sensed the effect our long conversation was having on me. "We've talked enough for today. I'm so happy to have found you. I can't wait to call Dawn and Noelle and tell them about you."

"I need to talk to them," I stated, with emphasis. I didn't want to lose another day.

Linda paused. "I'll give you their phone numbers, but why don't I have them call you later, maybe tomorrow. Don't you need a break?"

"Who do you think you are, my big sister?" I demanded, with false drama in my voice.

"Well, as a matter of fact I am." She sounded pleased with herself.

"So you're saying it's time for my nap?"

Linda barked out another deep laugh. "Don't argue with me." Of course, I didn't want to argue with her. I just wasn't ready to be sidetracked, even for a few hours. This was different, very different, from anything I had experienced before.

12

Despite Linda's maternal efforts to stage-manage my contacts with Dawn and Noelle that first day, the day I stopped being an only child, I raced to call them as soon as I'd re-lived Linda's call with Tibby. Dawn and Noelle may have been the two Throwaway sisters who grew up together, but my first telephone conversations with them left me wondering how they could be so different. Their Southern accents, and the photographs I would see a few days later, became my only early evidence that they were physically related. Born not much more than a year apart, they might have been mistaken for twins in their toddler-era photographs.

Noelle greeted me in our first call as an old friend, her noisy Southern-ness pounding across the telephone line. She wanted to tell me everything as quickly as possible. Her style masked a sensitivity that came through her corny joke-laden stories about her husband and kids, their struggles to survive recent financial setbacks, and her relationship with Sarah.

"So y'all are a big-shot lawyer, huh? And a Yankee, too?" It sounded to me like her accent was getting thicker with each word. She was enjoying the performance. "How could you have gone so wrong?"

"Wait a second," I sputtered. "I have to admit to being a lawyer, but I ain't no Yankee, ma'am." I had shifted into an exaggerated southern accent with a hint of Foghorn Leghorn, hoping to upstage hers. "Ah'll have yew know that ah was bawn in the capital of the Confederacy."

"Richmond?" she asked in a tone of playful contempt. "That was only the capital after it was taken away from Montgomery by old Jeff

Davis. Might as well have been born in New York City. Like claimin'
Washington is a Southern city just because it's below the Mason-Dixon
line."

I had to agree with her about Washington. The last time it might
have been a Southern town, it was still a swamp on the banks of the
Potomac.

"Wait just a minute," I protested. "I can even tell you which
Confederate generals died in battle by whether all of their horses'
hooves are on the ground in the statues along Monument Avenue."
My grandmother had pointed out the horses that were rearing back,
their forefeet off the ground, as we drove along Richmond's ceremonial
boulevard. "Don't I get some son-of-the-South points for that?"

Noelle wasn't ready to concede. "We'll just have to see whether
you measure up when you get here."

Tibby and I would be meeting her in Jacksonville over the
weekend.

* * *

Dawn was as cautious as her sister was open. Linda wanted me to
form my own opinions about our sisters, but had warned that Dawn
might be ambivalent about my arrival on the scene. I was another
opportunity to remind her of Sarah's abuse all those years before.

I had run at Dawn with all the enthusiasm I had gotten from her
sisters, but I could soon tell that she was not going to reveal much of
herself in our first call. She wasn't unfriendly, just not yet ready to
expose herself to this new brother in her life.

Dawn became more animated when she told me about her husband,
Jack, and their three sons and two daughters, who ranged in age from
fifteen to twenty-four. It sounded like they were a very tight family,
with all of the kids still close to home.

"Let's see," I started. "You have five kids and live in Salt Lake City.

You wouldn't happen to be Mormons, would you?" Linda had already told me they were.

Dawn laughed. "How could you guess? The kids run me ragged, and Jack is just as much of a kid himself. Someday one of them will learn to wash a dish." Her complaint was said in a way that suggested she was a willing martyr to her family.

"I thought all Mormon kids were supposed to be perfect," I said, drawing on my mental image of the unnaturally wholesome Osmond family.

"But perfect what? That's the question." Dawn's voice remained solemn in response; even her laughter was low-pitched and quiet.

I thought back to Linda's stern voice a couple of days before on our answering machine. But hers had quickly lightened as she engaged me in the story, and Noelle never seemed to have anything but fun in her voice. Dawn was going to be tougher to approach. I felt myself settling into a formal manner with her, not wanting to scare her away.

Her husband's telephone bear-hug only underscored Dawn's tentativeness. He had grabbed the phone from her hand near the end of our first call.

"Hey, fella." His voice was round and deep from his chest. "I can't tell you how much I've been lookin' forward to having you as a brother. I've been dealing with these three women all these years and need a guy on my side."

"I'm looking forward to it, too, Jack. Any chance you can come to D.C. with Dawn?" Linda and I were trying to set up a first meeting at my house. Dawn had been vague when I asked her about flying back east.

"Love to, absolutely love to," he insisted, "but I should stay and take care of the kids. Besides, this should just be you and the girls the first time around."

"Dawn didn't sound too sure about whether she could come." I suppose I wanted him to assure me that his wife was as eager to meet me as I was to meet her.

Jack seemed oblivious to my concern. "No problem. I got a million frequent flyer miles. She'll be there."

I could hear Dawn saying something in the background. Jack put his hand over the phone's mouthpiece, muffling their exchange. He came back on the line, sounding less confident. "I guess she has some rehearsals for her choral group that might get in the way."

Linda seemed to have expected Dawn's reaction. At least she didn't sound surprised when I told her that Dawn hadn't jumped at the chance to join us in Washington.

"Sounded to me like she was looking for excuses not to come," I said, trying to mask a growing sense of disappointment.

Linda became the big sister. "Don't worry about it. I'll call her."

"Don't make her do something she doesn't want to." I may have sounded hurt.

"Relax," Linda said, soothingly. "It's nothing personal. I got the same response the first time we talked. She's just trying to work things out in her mind right now. She'll be okay. Give it a day or two."

I could understand if Dawn was reluctant to find herself in a room with Sarah. But I was no ally of our birth mother. Why should I be damned by association? Linda was right, though: I couldn't take it personally. Dawn didn't know me well enough for her reaction to be about me.

* * *

I hadn't been able to tell my parents about finding Sarah or discovering that there were three Keepers in all, not just my older brother. The news would have been hard for them to understand, just as it had been for Tibby and me. My birth parents had no interest in becoming a part of my life. That made it easier to spare Mom and Dad what seemed like an unnecessary assault on their emotions. The arrival of my Throwaway sisters was an entirely different story; they made it impossible to continue the silence.

My mother had been anxious to help with my search. But I couldn't ignore her reaction when she had given me the adoption lawyer's name a year before. The two of us had been sitting at the dining-room table in my parents' house in Florida while Dad dozed in front of the TV in the living room.

It seemed to be Mom's favorite place to sit and talk; the small, wooden chairs fit her comfortably but dug into my gangly frame in the most annoying places. I was squirming as always, my impatience heightened by the need to get out of that chair-of-nails.

Mom had seemed on the verge of tears as she wrote out the lawyer's name on a slip of paper; that name seemed etched in her mind. The memory of our conversation was equally fixed in mine, despite the flood of events that had washed over me in the year since she had handed me that paper.

"What's wrong?" I had asked, squinting to see what I might have done to provoke tears.

"Nothing, really, I suppose." She sighed. "It's just that, well, I've always been afraid they'd come and take you away from us."

I laughed, trying to ease the moment. "Mom, I wouldn't fit in a basinet on the doorstep anymore," I reminded her. "They can't just come and carry me off."

"I'm being silly," she admitted. "I just can't help it." I reached over and squeezed her shoulder. She tried to smile, turning her head away so that I couldn't see her chin quivering and tears shining up in her eyes. "Do you remember the time your grandmother and I took you on a tour of the Virginia capitol building when you were, oh, probably ten years old?"

"Sure," I agreed. Not really.

"In the central hall of the Capitol, the walls are filled with oil paintings of all of the governors of Virginia," she recalled, setting the scene. "I was startled when you spent a long time looking at the paintings, sometimes getting right up against the picture, as if you were really looking for something."

I could pull images of the Capitol from my memory, but not the governors' portraits. "I've always been interested in looking at artists' brush strokes, probably from all those years watching you paint," I reminded her. "There couldn't have been anything deeper on my mind." Mom had used her talent as a portrait artist to make a few extra dollars when my thirty-nine-year-old father decided to go to college right after I was born. The pungent aroma of turpentine and oil paints is an indelible memory from my childhood.

My attention to the governors' portraits a few years later had meant nothing. But my mother, who knew of my descent from Governor Wise long before I did, had not been so sure: "I was afraid you'd see yourself staring out of one of those paintings. I don't know what I would have done then."

13

Tibby and I cancelled a vacation planned around my fortieth birthday, now just a few days away. I tried to sound casual on the phone call to my parents, but I'm sure my voice betrayed my nervousness.

"We'd like to come down next weekend to celebrate my fortieth with you and Dad. Would that be okay?" Not entirely truthful, but the best I could do under the circumstances.

"Wonderful!" She was surprised and excited. I was ashamed at my selfishness for needing a reason to visit.

During the week that followed, I had to act like a lawyer even though my mind was filled with the possibilities presented by my new family. I was also coming to terms with how much of my new circumstances should be public and how much kept private. The new version of my adoption story didn't feel like something I wanted to hide. I cautiously allowed myself to be happy about the events that were overtaking me.

That first day after talking to Linda, Noelle, and Dawn, I sat in my new law firm trying to contain the emotions that had kept me awake most of the night before. The friend who had just convinced me to move to the firm popped her head through the door at mid-morning.

"What's up?" Mandy Sellen had been very attentive following my arrival, in part to prove that my last experience with the airless law firm wouldn't be repeated.

I wasn't sure what the next phase of my life would be like, but I was certain that Mandy deserved to know why her friend might be distracted. It hadn't sunk into me yet how much my new siblings might change my world.

"We need to talk," I began. I slowly started telling her what had been going on over the last few months. I heard the shortness of breath in my voice that was a tell-tale sign of nervousness, but I was warming to the storytelling, using it to work things out for myself as I talked. Mandy's face often mirrored the expression of the person with whom she was talking, and now it reflected the excitement I was feeling.

"There you have it," I concluded, trying to sound lawyer-neutral. "What do you think?" Mandy was the first outsider to hear about my new family. I was genuinely interested in her reaction.

She sat for a moment, then began to speak softly. "I have three sisters and I love all of them. But we have a lifetime of baggage to deal with. Now you have three new sisters and you'll get to know and love them for who they are today. It's a great gift."

* * *

When I moved into the law firm, I didn't realize that my new office was a minefield. It overlooked a dramatic stretch of Pennsylvania Avenue between the White House and the Capitol. From my windows you could see in the distance a sliver of the Potomac River as you looked past the National Archives, the National Gallery of Art, and, across the broad expanse of the Mall, the Smithsonian's National Air and Space Museum. Washington is a city of low buildings closely set together, so most desk-bound guys spend their working lives staring out windows across thirty-foot alleys into the windows of other desk-bound guys. I had lucked into the best view I was likely to have as a Washington lawyer.

Office politics had somehow declared my room a no-man's-land for all of the existing partners in the firm. If one of them wasn't going to have that office, none of them would. I heard something to that effect from each of the partners who had coveted the office, although the villains were too varied for me to keep straight so early in my new existence.

Most law firms make the partners buy their own office furniture, so my move included carting my old furniture along with me. I was the modern equivalent of the desert Bedouin, setting up a new practice in a new place while sitting at the same desk with the same junk (maybe a little less dusty because of the move) in the same desk drawers, and the same books and deal mementos on the bookshelves.

Ignorant of the events to come, a week earlier I had arranged a grueling day of telephone interviews. I needed to interrogate, gingerly, some of the most senior executives of my biggest client, a giant manufacturing company under investigation for possible criminal violations of the obscure laws that had become my life. A partner in our Boston main office joined me on the phone for back-to-back interviews of the executives as they came onto and dropped off the line from wherever they were around the country. The interviews would take most of the day, with little time for breaks in between. Only obsessive lawyers would concoct such a routine.

The day of the call had unfortunately become the second day after Linda's first contact with me. I was talking into the speakerphone at my desk as I led a vice president through the drill of questions that probably felt to him like the cross-examinations he had seen on television. I kept my questions as precise as I could, trying to signal the gravity of the situation without causing panic in the executive suite of the company. Clients seem to need their lawyers to be imposing figures, and they certainly want them to display clarity of thought and seriousness of purpose.

I was in mid-question when a messenger pushed his way into my office, walked quickly across the room, and dropped a box in front of me. I hadn't been expecting anything, but the life of a modern lawyer seemed to be filled with unexpected, and often unwanted, packages.

Without looking at the address label, I absent-mindedly yanked the cardboard strip along the edge of the box and tipped the contents onto the desk in front of me. A dozen clear, zip-lock plastic bags filled with photographs spilled out, post-it notes stuck to each bag: "Our sister Dawn and her husband Jack," "Noelle's kids," "my adoptive family, Christmas '65."

It hit me: I was looking at my birth family. I splayed the packages across the table with both hands, trying to decide which present to open first. I studied the resulting montage of faces staring up at me through the plastic. Did I look enough like any of these people to be one of them? After all those years of not knowing where I came from, it was hard to accept the truth. Was it possible that I wasn't who Linda thought I was? The bitter taste from my contacts with Sarah lingered, sowing doubt about the happy ending that Linda was trying to orchestrate.

I opened the bags at random, flipping over each photo to see what clues someone might have written about the smiling relatives on the other side. There were enough pictures showing variations on the dark hair, thin face, and long neck I saw reflected in the mirror that I began to believe that my photograph might have a place among them.

The images sucked me in, until reality intruded. How long had I been staring at the pictures? My ears recognized that the executive on the other end of the line was still talking. I sagged with relief. It sounded like he was responding to the last question I remembered asking. I forced myself to stop looking at the pictures.

A hard day became torture. Who cared what these corporate guys had to say? I could have been studying the faces of my sisters, their kids, their adoptive parents. There were even a few aged snapshots of Sarah, Dan, and the Keepers that the resourceful Linda had managed to get her hands on over the years.

My Boston partner and I signed off the phone line at the end of the marathon interviews. He immediately called back to compare notes on what we thought we had accomplished. I cut him off: "I need a little time to regroup."

He responded sarcastically: "Go take a leak and call me back."

"No, it's not that. Something happened in the middle of our call, when I was questioning Peter Falon. Did I seem okay to you?"

My partner, a no-nonsense guy, must have thought I was fishing for compliments. "Yeah, yeah. Great job," he said sourly.

I should have kept my performance anxiety to myself, but now I needed to come clean or leave my new colleague with the impression that I was a fool. I gave him the five-minute tour of the last couple of days, ending with the delivery of the photographs in mid-interview.

"What's wrong with you?" My partner seemed angry.

"Excuse me?" Maybe I should have kept my mouth shut. Telling him seemed to have annoyed him even more.

"Are you out of your mind?" he asked, although now with a softer tone. "If this had happened to me, I'd have blown off these interviews so fast. No, wait. I wouldn't even have remembered they were supposed to happen. I'd be running down the street telling everybody, having fun with it. Where's your perspective, moron?"

I wondered whether I *was* a moron. Why didn't I just step back and enjoy the moment?

* * *

A cheery yellow envelope sat in the midst of all the bags of hastily arranged photos. Its handwritten inscription said: "Open this first."

"This" was an early clue to my sister Linda's personality. Inside was a birthday card—my first from a sister, everything being firsts these days—and inside that was a stack of photographs of Linda at various phases of her life.

Half the pictures showed her, a beautiful woman, in outrageous (and sometimes politically incorrect) Halloween costumes, an obvious enthusiasm. But the last in the pile was a forlorn shot of a little kid slumped in a stroller, sulking under clown face-paint. A mom is bent over the stroller, face away from the camera and butt toward it. She's hugely overweight, a fact made more painful by the strain her rear end is putting on the fabric of the unflattering print dress that's hiked up to show her thick legs to their worst effect. Someone had drawn an arrow toward the woman. On the back of the picture, in the same ink, were the words: "I've put on a few pounds so don't be surprised when you see me."

I called Linda that night, after sweeping the photos into my briefcase and hurrying home to show them to Tibby. My sister asked immediately: "Did you get the pictures?"

"Of course I got the pictures," I shouted into the phone, for dramatic effect. "You nearly destroyed my career." She laughed as I described the results of her surprise delivery.

I went from bag to bag as Linda slowly took me through the photographs of my birth parents, siblings, nieces, and nephews. We lingered over fuzzy shots of Sarah as a young woman and Dan in his Korean War uniform. I saw nothing of myself in Sarah's solemn stare into the camera. It was easier to find me in Dan's image; his narrow face, dark eyes, and hair reflected mine. A picture of my twenty-year-old brother Greg showed the same angular face, but he looked much more like the athlete I wasn't, with a huskier physique. At least I hadn't been forced to stumble behind a jock brother through my school years. I squinted to imagine what Greg might look like today. I doubted that he would be enough like me to have been picked out as my subway-riding twin.

"Do you have more pictures of Sarah and Dan?" The few she had sent of my birth mother seemed almost surreptitious, as if the photographer knew she would have objected to posing. An odd shot of

Dan, taken at close range, showed him lying on his back on a made bed, his head tilted up by a stack of pillows so that he could read the book perched open on his chest. He frowned at the camera, a cigarette dangling from his mouth.

"That's pretty much it. I was surprised when she gave me those. Sarah claims to hate having her picture taken. She says she's so ugly."

"Dan doesn't look all that happy, either," I responded quickly. "At least not in this picture of him on the bed."

"He looked good in his military picture," Linda said brightly, as if sticking up for our birth father. "I think he was supposed to be quite a catch for Sarah. I sent the bed shot because that's the last one I have of him." Now her tone shifted to a resigned monotone. "And I get the sense from Sarah that that's the way to picture him these days, hanging out in his room, reading, and smoking. Almost a hermit."

I set aside the photographs of our birth parents, moving on to the happy faces of Linda, Dawn, and Noelle's families. Most of the shots were traditional groupings at holidays, graduations, or weddings. I watched babies become teenagers from one frame to the next, some of them my sisters, others my sisters' children. A few pictures showed the memories that built families: Dawn had five kids; in one photograph her three boys posed, teenaged, bare-chested, and embarrassed. All of their visible skin, except for comical sunglass circles around their eyes, was fireball red from a day spent ignoring their parents' warnings on a Hawaiian beach.

Linda laughed. "Jack, he's Dawn's husband and a real sweetheart, forced the boys to stand still for that picture as a future reminder of what happens when they don't listen to their parents about putting on suntan lotion." I began to wonder if I could ever expect to be a real part of these families. They already had so many memories without me.

The largest picture in the dozens Linda had sent was of her, one of those eight-by-ten school photographs our parents were forced to buy to show that they were good parents and we were forced to sit for when the last thing we wanted was a permanent record of how awkward we looked. "Awkward" is the kindest word I could apply to the stern twelve-year-old staring into that schoolhouse camera. Tons of freckles, red hair pulled back behind her ears, and a pair of those cat-eye glasses that formed wings extending out from the wearer's eyebrows, so unstylish that they're almost trendy today. I could accept that the photo's subject could transform into the beautiful Linda in the later pictures, but mostly because I hoped I didn't resemble the goofy kid in my pictures from the same era.

"Uh, Linda," I began, struggling to sound sincere. "I'm looking at a big photo of you that's dated September 1964 on the back." Dramatic pause. "Nice picture."

"Like it?" Linda barked. "I call that my 'keep-her-in-the-attic-so-the-neighbors-won't-know phase,' but I felt you needed to see the bad as well as the good."

"When do I get to see 'the good'?" I asked, sarcasm back in control of my voice.

"Shut up. By the way, what did you think of the pictures inside the birthday card?" Linda was trying to act nonchalant.

"Great costumes," I admitted. I had always avoided costume parties, but it looked like my bias wasn't a hereditary trait. "Aunt Jemima seemed risky, but you made a great Wonder Woman."

"That was a few years ago." My sister sighed, a bit over-dramatically. "I don't look quite the same now."

I decided to take a gamble, as I was reasonably sure that the fat-butt photo was a hoax. "I especially liked the shot of you and—gotta be Matt, right?—Matt in the stroller. I know I shouldn't say this, you being my sister and all, but I really like big women, so your current look is great."

Pause. "Aw, come on. Didn't I have you going at least for a minute?

I love that picture."

"You mean it's not you?" I responded, equally over-dramatically. "I'm crushed. Who is that spectacular woman?"

"Okay, okay. Don't be such a wise guy," she growled. I smiled to myself. Linda and I had known each other for only two days, if we could even say that we knew each other yet. But we already had an easy rapport, the ability to engage in a comfortable dialogue without concern for formalities.

Linda was enjoying the story. "We were on one of those God-awful field trips to the zoo for one of the kids' schools and I was in my take-a-million-pictures phase. I saw that little kid with the face-paint sitting there looking annoyed and I thought it was funny, so I snapped a shot."

My sister launched another of her bark-laughs. "It was only when I had the roll developed that I realized I had mostly photographed that woman's butt. That dumb picture's been floating around for years and I stumbled on it while I was grabbing pictures to send you."

I laughed, then sighed noisily. Linda laughed back. "Get used to it," she said firmly. I looked forward to getting used to this engaging sister I hadn't known existed barely an instant before.

* * *

Mom and Dad insisted on picking us up at the Orlando airport the next Saturday morning. I felt like a squirmy seven-year-old as we drove the thirty minutes to the house where I had grown up. Tibby and I agreed that we would wait until after lunch to break the news. We had used the last five days to absorb the new reality, study the pictures of our new family, and talk on the phone every night with my new sisters. Now all we had to do was convey those events in the right light to my parents.

Mom is a meticulous housekeeper and gardener. Our home was a typical one-story, cinderblock affair; everything in Florida seems to be built out of cinderblock, just about the only building material the bugs won't eat. It was made handsome by her constant effort.

Her parents were both remarkable gardeners. Grandmother tended her finicky, ancient boxwoods with skill, while my grandfather turned the acre plot surrounding their house in a fine old Richmond neighborhood into a true working farm. As a kid I remember playing in the rows of tall corn and picking strawberries and raspberries during hot summers. Summer was a time of ripe tomatoes and peas freshly shelled from their pods; everything at the table seemed to come from within the boundaries of my grandfather's urban dream. Early fall would find him high on a ladder deep in the apple trees, picking the last, the best, of the season's fruit. Those moments are on the shortlist of memories I wish I could recapture, if only to be sure that I had appreciated them at the time for how extraordinary they were.

*   *   *

Mom began to clear the table after lunch. Tibby nervously nodded her head when I raised my eyebrows at her. "Mom and Dad," I started, "I have some really good news." I began with Linda's call the weekend before, speaking in a slow monotone. I didn't want them to think I was too excited by events that they might translate as somehow pushing them aside. They sat quietly at first, but quickly showed their excitement. It *was* good news to them.

Mom assaulted us with questions. At first they were the fun ones about the three women I hadn't known less than a week before. My parents would eventually spend hours on the phone with all three of my new sisters. But Mom also needed to understand Sarah Jones, the woman who had given them a child. "You talked to her on the phone?" she asked tentatively.

I had been vague about my contacts with Sarah. It still felt like disloyalty to have approached her.

"Twice," I confessed. "She wasn't so nice the first time." No need to get into those details; Mom wouldn't take them well. "But she called me back and was much better."

"Did she tell you why?"

"Why?"

"Why it all happened," my mother clarified. "Why they gave you and the others up for adoption." We all wanted to know why.

"No. She didn't tell me much about anything, really. I didn't feel like I could ask a lot of questions."

"It must have been very sad for her. You need to tell her that I want to thank her for what she did for us."

"I don't expect to talk to her again, at least not anytime soon," I answered, trying not to show how little I relished the thought. "I think I've gotten everything I need from her."

"But what about her husband and children, your brother and the two sisters?" Mom asked, showing the same frustration I had felt after my last contact with Sarah.

"If you believe Sarah, Dan Jones doesn't admit we're alive," I explained. "And the Keepers…."

"The Keepers?" Mom looked confused.

"That's what I call Sarah's three official children, as opposed to us Throwaways," I admitted.

Mom looked stricken. "Don't talk like that. You weren't thrown away."

I laughed. "Sure I was. I was just lucky that you and Dad were there to catch me." I thought to myself that I probably shouldn't keep using the Keeper and Throwaway labels, at least not around my parents. "Anyway, the Keepers are a mystery. We have no idea what they know and don't know."

"All that matters right now is that you have your sisters…." Mom teared up in mid-sentence.

Dad growled: "What are you crying about? This is a wonderful thing."

Mom blotted her eyes with a tissue she had been clutching tightly in her hand. "I know," she said. "I'm very happy. For all these years I've worried that when we died David and Tibby would be all alone. Now I know they won't be."

14

Tibby hated flying in small planes. She had spent most of her childhood in South America at a time when Third World air travel often meant unwanted adventures in aviation. She displayed her best sportsmanship as we boarded the ten-passenger propjet for the twenty-minute flight from Orlando to Jacksonville.

I wanted the four Throwaways together in one place, but Linda hinted that Noelle and her husband, Andy, shouldn't be asked to spend money flying to Washington. A detour from Orlando to Jacksonville had become the best alternative, but I wasn't convinced that this cautious diplomacy was necessary. I knew how to act with strangers and casual acquaintances, but not the rules for dealing with older sisters I had never met before. Forget whether she likes milk in her coffee. I lacked even the basics most forty-year-old men would know about their sister.

Noelle, the middle sister, would be waiting for us at the airport. I leaned across the aisle of the narrow airplane toward Tibby, raising my voice over the noise of the engines: "This feels weird."

Tibby looked up from her book. "What's wrong?" She was sure I was talking about a wing falling off the plane. She gripped her book tightly, probably reading the same page throughout the flight, willing the plane to stay in the air at the same time.

I smiled at her tense stare. "Not the plane, Sweetdog," I reassured her. "Meeting a sister we didn't even know I had a week ago."

Tibby visibly relaxed, turning to look out the window on her side of the plane, satisfying herself that at least one of the propellers continued to spin. She twisted back toward me, stretching to talk into my ear. "It is sort of surreal, no? And I don't have much of a sense of Noelle yet, at least not like Linda." Tibby was delighted by Linda, who seemed to fill more of the expectations we had built up for my brother over the years. Noelle was more of an unknown. My wife was anxious to get back to D.C. and meet Linda and Dawn the following weekend.

"Don't you suppose Noelle must feel the same way?" I mumbled almost to myself, trying to imagine Noelle's expectations for me. "It has to be odd. We're both taking a risk." In a few minutes I would actually touch my first blood relative, so I was ready to take the chance. I had been so caught up in the events of the past week that I hadn't dwelled on what was really happening: Three women that I wouldn't have recognized on the street had fallen into my life. It felt like a good thing, but was that only because I wasn't thinking critically enough?

I looked over and caught Tibby's eye. "You're okay with this, right?" She gave me a thin smile, the kind that could have been saying anything from "It's too late for that now" to "All I care about is getting off this plane," and went back to her book. I shifted in my seat, trying to find a way to extract my knees from the seatback in front of me. A cloudless sky let my mind wander off into a study of the coastline 10,000 feet below.

* * *

We taxied off the runway toward the gate. I stared out the little porthole, straining to look up at the windows of the terminal for a face something like mine. I was nervous and excited, maybe scared. Would I cry? Not my style, but this was virgin territory.

The little commuter plane was too small for a jetway, so we had to climb out and walk across the tarmac to stairs leading up to the boarding area. Noelle would see me first if she was pressed up against the window as I know I would have been. I hoped I wouldn't be a disappointment after all her years of looking for me.

Noelle's husband had been videotaping our arrival through the window. When I saw the tape later, Noelle's voice provided an off-camera review of the passengers as they climbed down from the plane. She sounded as tense as I had been: "Can't be him; too short. Come on, lady, get off the plane. Look! That's got to be him. Tall. Dark hair. Yep. That's him." She was right; on screen I had ducked to get through the plane's low doorway, following Tibby down the short ladder. Noelle chattered nervously as we crossed the pavement and climbed the next flight of stairs at the end of the empty jetway.

We came through the gate doorway and instantly spotted my sister, a tall, handsome women with short brown hair and a big smile. She grabbed me with a "Whoop!" and tears in her eyes. Her husband pointed the video camera at us awkwardly, seeming unsure whether his role should be videographer or new brother-in-law.

My face flushed as I hugged my sister. I looked over her shoulder at Tibby, who stood silently, smiling broadly a few steps back. My sister and I pulled away from each other, stammering into disjointed conversation. Andy stopped filming, saying that he wasn't sure he knew how to operate "the dang camera," and thrust a plastic-wrapped bouquet of flowers into my hand. I gave the flowers a confused stare and handed them to Tibby.

I noticed an elderly woman standing on the other side of the corridor outside the gate area. She seemed to be watching the proceedings with rapt attention. Could this be Noelle's adoptive mother? I didn't want to be rude to a new relative, especially one who might be apprehensive about this latest turn of events. I looked at Noelle and cocked my head toward the woman.

My sister followed my gaze and laughed. "I don't have any idea who she is," she whispered. "I've been making such a scene for the last half-hour about how nervous I was to be meeting my brother. I'm surprised there isn't a bigger crowd." I smiled, attempting a suave nod at the woman with my best Cary Grant imitation. She waved sheepishly and turned away as if she hadn't really been staring at us in the first place.

Noelle had been holding up a banner as I walked into the waiting area. It had fallen to the ground during our hug. She bent down and spread it out for me to read. I had been too focused on her to take in the message: "Happy 1st Birthday, Brand New Baby Brother! May 23, 1995." My fortieth had been the day before, but my first birthday was today as far as my new big sister was concerned.

We began to walk toward baggage claim. "I have to warn you in advance about the van," Noelle said. "That piece of junk might not get us back to Amelia Island, might not even start. But it's the only thing big enough to get the four of us and your luggage out to the island. And my car isn't in much better shape, sorry to say."

"Sounds fine to me." I didn't suggest that we could have rented a car, even if the idea of pushing a van out of an airport parking garage wasn't appealing. Noelle wanted to take care of us, and she had made enough joking references to me as a fancy lawyer that I had to avoid acting like one.

"Y'all are going to stay at a condo I borrowed at the resort," she informed us cautiously. I must have looked surprised, assuming that we were going to stay with her and her family. Noelle laughed self-consciously. "Andy's a pack rat; the house is a mess. Y'all will be more comfortable in the condo."

"I don't care what your house looks like," I said quickly. Noelle began to respond, then stopped. She didn't know how to talk to her new brother. I took her off the hook: "I've heard that the resort is great. It'll be fun to stay there, as long as we're hanging out with you." She smiled and the worry in her face softened.

The van started without drama. As we drove out of the airport, I studied Noelle while she talked non-stop to Tibby about how we would fill the next day and a half together. She had a nose shaped like mine, except for the Roman bump on the bridge of hers. My bump was missing as the result of a nose job following an accident in eighth-grade gym class. Five years my senior, Noelle probably would have been out of the house and no longer my protector—or tormentor—when at fourteen I had come home from school broken-nosed and swollen-faced.

That she could have been my tormentor was clear as we squared off that night in the borrowed condo for my first arm-wrestling competition with a woman. Andy proudly warned that his wife was even stronger than she looked, goading me to take on the challenge. I gallantly offered to wrestle with my right hand; I was left-handed and stronger on that side. We grabbed each other's hand, put our elbows on the glass-topped table and jockeyed for position.

I yelled, "Keep your elbow on the table." No idea what that was all about. Did I really need the contest to comply with the rules?

Andy pointed his camera at us and shouted "Go!" The videotape later showed shock spreading over my face. I jumped up as I finally pulled Noelle's arm to the table, stunned that I had to work so hard. "*Out-rage-ous!*" I roared. "I can't believe it. You *are* strong!"

Noelle looked down at the floor, whining: "But you didn't even use your stronger arm." She had expected to win. I liked my first exercise in sibling rivalry, and not just because I had won. This was going to be fun, particularly now that I wasn't the scrawny kid being abused by his big sister.

That was an aspect of this later-in-life adventure that intrigued me. My three new sisters and I had converged at a point where our age differences were immaterial. We had missed a lifetime of good and bad memories together, but were spared the misperceptions that come from applying childhood prejudices to adult actions. Maybe our relationships would develop differently in the void.

* * *

Noelle and I continued to play brother-sister games, trying to map the territory. She was sitting across the dinner table from me, absent-mindedly pushing through the piles of family photographs Andy had pulled out of boxes. I had spotted her low-heeled shoes under the dinner table between us, where she had kicked them off earlier in the evening in preparation for the arm-wrestling event.

"Hey, whose shoes are these?" I asked. "They look like size twelves." My shoe size. I looked at Andy. "Don't think these are yours. Red's not your color."

"Very funny," Noelle said in a self-conscious tone from the other side of the table. She slid down in her chair, reaching her left toe to hook one of the shoes. I stretched out my leg and kicked the shoes away from her, then nudged them toward me. I pulled off my shoes and struggled to twist my feet into hers. It was less of a struggle than Noelle probably would have wanted.

She jumped up and came around the table toward me. I stood up and wobbled away from her, trying to walk in the tight shoes. "Those cost me a bunch. Better not stretch them out."

"Actually they feel kind of loose. Maybe they're more like thir-teens?" Noelle punched my shoulder, bent down to grab my shoes from where I'd dropped them, then hopped around as she put one foot, then the other, into my loafers.

She stopped sharply, standing with the distant look of a woman considering the fit of the pair the shoe salesman has just slipped on her feet. Then she laughed loudly. "Gotta admit. These feel more comfort-able than mine."

Later we moved on to comparing skills at touching our noses with our tongues (*her* tongue to *her* nose; *my* tongue to *my* nose). I even took on the role of the family lawyer, listening to Andy's tale of the litigation he was about to file over his politically motivated firing as director of mosquito control for the island. My desire to fit into the family overrode my experienced judgment as I offered legal advice on a problem, and to a brother-in-law, mostly unknown to me.

Then I turned nervously to mixing it up with Noelle's three teenaged sons. I'd had limited contact with teenagers since the time I was one myself, and I doubted that I would be a gifted communicator with these boys, or any boys between the ages of fourteen and eighteen. Noelle's stories over the phone suggested that her youngest was a rebellious kid flirting with trouble and that her oldest was quietly adrift.

Sean, the oldest and quietest, glanced away whenever I tried to look him in the eyes. Randy's straight brown hair ran to his shoulder blades; he wore his baseball cap backwards and had on an oversized tee-shirt glorifying a heavy-metal band. Randy seemed like a personable kid, full of ambitious plans for himself. Noelle hoped he would keep moving toward college. The youngest boy, Jason, had surprised his parents the day before with a shaved head. He was pleased with his gaunt, death-camp look, particularly after seeing his parents' reaction.

I tried to imagine what it would be like, as a teenager, to meet my mother's adult little brother for the first time. I was having a hard enough time, as a grown man, figuring out what it was like to meet my sisters. The boys' initial reaction was to study me, silently and wide-eyed, as if I were a mutant lab rat. I assumed that typical teenage reticence around adults would be intensified by the circumstances, but they warmed quickly and were open to my over-anxious interrogations. I had once again retreated into my role as the information-starved lawyer to avoid the silence of an intimidating situation.

Noelle watched the process intently from across the room. I couldn't decide whether she was waiting to jump in and pull me out of danger if things started going badly or hovering in fear that her sons might say something embarrassing. It was neither. She eventually

clapped her hands and announced that she was taking her baby brother
for a walk on the beach.

As the boys wandered off, she whispered to me, "Child, you got
them to tell you things I could never drag out of them. Sean sounds
more interested in that girl than I thought. Come down here more
often so I can learn what they're up to." I wasn't sure that I had gotten
anything revealing out of the boys, but I had engaged them momentarily. That might have been as much as a mother could hope for under
the circumstances.

* * *

Late that night we sat at a table in Noelle's kitchen eating birthday
cake, what Noelle kept describing as my "first birthday cake." I was
sure that the kitchen event had been moved at the last moment from
the fancy condo to reassure me that they didn't live in a shanty.

It looked like a nice house to me. There was no evidence of Andy's
yard sale collections, whatever those might be. It was too dark to see
whether he had really turned the backyard into a cemetery for rusting
semi-trailers, but I still sneaked a glimpse out a window on my way to
the bathroom. I needed my own evidence to decide whether my sister
was exaggerating her husband's eccentricity.

We were looking at the typical, hastily composed photographs of
her family at play when Noelle looked up at the kitchen clock. "Lord,
it's almost midnight," she shouted. "I gotta be up at four to get to
the lab by six." She worked odd hours as a lab technician at the local
hospital, delaying her ambitions to develop real estate or open a small
business.

Andy yawned sourly, stretching his arms over his head. "And I
get to sleep in until six." He worked part-time at the island's seaport,
waiting for his litigation against the local politicians to meander
through the process.

I didn't have much in common with my sister and her family, but I wanted to. I would have to learn how to be a brother and uncle, not just a celebrity guest.

15

few days later Tibby and I were at another airport. This time
we were the ones waiting for a plane to arrive, but still weren't
the ones videotaping the event. My new sister Linda sat on
the plane with her camera rolling, shooting the interior of the plane
and then talking nervously to the lens about meeting her brother in
a few minutes. When Linda played the tape for me later, I couldn't
imagine that I would ever have pointed a video camera at myself and
recorded an unself-conscious monologue, much less shown the tape to
the subject of the monologue.

My first glimpse of Linda in person was of a tall redhead whose face
was obscured by the video camera filming me seeing her for the first
time. Her camera became a fixture over the next few days, along with
her easy laughter. It didn't take long to understand where Linda's place
would have been in the big family that never was: She would have been
the smart, wise-guy prankster. I'm not sure whether she would have
been my greatest ally or stiffest opponent. Now adversarial positioning
was out of the question. I was the brother she had worried she would
never find; she was the sister who had worked so hard to find me.

We grabbed Linda's luggage and rushed to another airport across
town to pick up Dawn, flying in from Salt Lake City. The few pictures
I had seen of Dawn were professional shots, literally of the beauty-
queen variety. She had been crowned Mrs. Illinois and Mrs. Utah in
the early 1980s. But she still looked enough like her younger self that
I recognized her easily through the crowd at the gate. She smiled
cautiously as she caught sight of us. And that was the sense I had of

her throughout the weekend ahead. She seemed happy to be with us, but hesitant. I had been surprised when Jack, Dawn's husband, had called to tell me that everything was arranged for her trip. That call had been preceded by back-and-forth with Dawn about why she shouldn't leave Salt Lake just then.

I checked myself: Was my early sense of Dawn more prejudice than reality, some underlying sensitivity to her conservative Mormon ties? She made only passing references to the church, and I probably raised the topic more than she did. Dawn sang professionally with the Mormon Tabernacle Choir and other groups. Music was important to her, and I wanted to understand that part of her life. It seemed like a safe window through which to get to know her better.

I've never been deeply impressed with organized religion, and generally feel ill-at-ease around those who are, so I consciously worked to set aside the broad biases that might skew our relationship. I also tried a little harder to keep my language G-rated.

Dawn seemed reluctant to open up to me in the way that had felt instinctive with Linda and Noelle. I looked to Linda, who had known Dawn and Noelle for years now, for signals on how to gauge my early interactions with Dawn.

Linda sat in the kitchen sipping a can of diet Seven-Up, apparently her morning addiction, when I came downstairs early the morning after the girls' arrival. "You found the Seven-Up. Sure that's all you want?" I asked. Not my idea of breakfast.

Linda had been dreamily staring at nothing. She turned, sleepy-eyed, toward me. "You guys were so sweet to stock up. You didn't have to."

"Tibby was the clever one. I guess you said something to her about that particular, revolting breakfast choice. Just be sure to drink it all up before you leave." I had already made her eating habits a theme of my teasing.

I kept going. "Do you want some more of that Andre's fake Champagne to pour in it?" At dinner the night before, Linda preferred the cheap bubbles to the wine we offered; Dawn had stuck with water. Tibby had been pleased with herself as she stocked the refrigerator with uncharacteristic choices.

"Leave my Andre's alone," she ordered. "It's worth every penny of the three dollars you spent on it."

I looked at Linda with an arched eyebrow, signaling a change of subject. "Dawn's kinda quiet. Is that always the way she's been with you, or is something else going on?"

"She's pretty reserved, just like me." She looked up at me, batting her eyelashes coquettishly.

I snorted. "Right. So that's just the way she is?"

Linda rocked her head from side to side, measuring what she wanted to say next. "I think she's still got a lot of resentment toward Sarah. It brings back bad memories for her, us sitting around talking about all this stuff."

"We can't exactly ignore it." My words came out more forcefully than I'd intended.

"Of course not. Some part of you wants to say 'get over it' to her, but it is what it is. And Dawn is *definitely* quieter than Noelle and me." Linda stopped and looked at me for effect. "At least she's not as much of a stiff as you are." She tried to poke me in the side with an index finger but I dodged out of the way.

I probably *was* more like Dawn than Linda in how I related to people, or held back from them. So it felt pleasantly out of character as I let myself fall into the communal role of little brother to these women. The last morning we were together, Linda and Dawn had come into the kitchen with their hair up in pink, spongy curlers. They had soon yanked my short hair around some of the curlers.

"Ouch," I yelled, faking pain from the hair pulling.

Dawn pulled harder. "Be quiet," she demanded. "I'm working."

"Yeah," Linda snarled. "We didn't get to use you as a doll when you were a year old. Pay your dues." By the time they were finished, I felt like one of those stoic Labrador Retrievers you see wearing a hat, sunglasses, and a pack of kids on its tail.

I decided that I could have some fun, too. "Hey, Dawn. Did I tell you what a friend said when he saw your picture?"

"Nooo, what?" She knew she was being set up.

"He said you looked like me in drag," a pathetic tone to my voice. She pretended outrage, but giggled as I continued. "I told him that was ridiculous. I would look much better than *that* as a girl."

"Wait a second!" Linda jumped into the conversation, ready to defend her sister against the new kid.

Tibby joined in as well, wagging a finger in the air. "I know how to settle this." She walked into the living room and pulled a copy of my ancient high-school yearbook off the shelf. I knew what she intended to find.

"Here, Dawn. Check this out." Tibby dropped the yearbook on the kitchen counter and flipped quickly through it until she hit the unfortunate page. Sliding the open book along the counter toward Dawn, she said solemnly, "I think you look a lot better."

A service club to which I belonged in school had held an annual fund-raiser. Someone had decided it would be funny if the all-male group put on a fashion show for the school, featuring only women's fashions. High school was meant to teach us about bad ideas and how to avoid them in the future.

The yearbook photo shows me from the waist up, blouse marginally constraining an overstuffed bra, looking at least something like one of my sisters. A girl had studiously applied my makeup backstage before the performance. I had wanted garish lipstick and eye shadow to leave no subtlety about the farce; she unfortunately did a stylish job of it. One of the other guys in the show had stopped and slowly checked me out, from wobbly high heels to long black wig. In a thoughtful tone he had said: "Not bad. I'd ask you out if you weren't so tall."

Linda grabbed the yearbook. "I gotta have a copy of this photo." She was enjoying the moment.

Dawn stared solemnly at the picture, trying to find something better to say than her grudging admission: "I guess we do look a lot alike."

I glanced past Dawn at Tibby. I wondered if she found all of this as disconcerting and wonderful as I did, playing with two women I barely knew as if they were family. They were family and strangers at the same time. This felt so intimate to me, but I wondered whether a casual observer might have seen our interactions as nothing special. I had no baseline, nothing against which to judge my emotions.

Tibby smiled and winked at me as she reached over to straighten one of the pink curlers in my hair. I grabbed her hand and pulled her away from Linda and Dawn, who were now bent over my yearbook, flipping through the pages for other incriminating evidence to use against me. "Are you having fun?" I asked.

She seemed surprised by the question. "Of course. Shouldn't I be?"

I looked with satisfaction toward my sisters, who were razzing the 1973 hairstyles of my classmates. "Ready to add crazy sisters to the mix?"

She smiled. "Now you ask?"

My eyes jumped from Linda and Dawn back to Tibby. Was there more than her tone suggested?

She must have seen the question in my face, and shook her head with a smile. "This is great. I just have to get used to it."

* * *

My sisters' visit gave me confidence to broaden the circle of friends who heard our story. A happy ending seemed to be developing. Telling the story became an important piece of who I was, or who I wanted to present to the world. A surprising number of people responded with revelations of their own, sometimes the discovery that one of their parents had been married before (or not) and had produced a half-sister or -brother, other times a wrenching childhood experience.

My story seemed so often to tap an empathetic nerve in friends and acquaintances, revealing a different side to their personalities, that I wondered what I had failed to see in them in the past. I needed an antidote for my self-involvement.

I sat at my desk one morning talking on the phone to a client, telling her the abbreviated version of my birthday surprise and the Throwaway reunions over the past week. Sandy, always a high-energy, fast talker with lots of noisy opinions about everything, had little to say during my monologue. Most people interrupted enthusiastically with the same questions. I had expected more than the random "uh huhs" I had gotten from her. Now she had gone completely silent.

I paused in the storytelling. "Sandy, are you still there?" More silence. "Sandy?"

In a tiny voice: "I'm here. I've just been thinking about things I tried to put out of my mind a long time ago."

What had I done now? I had heard ice in the voices of a couple of adoptive parents who weren't sure whether they liked the idea of birth families reappearing and reuniting. Maybe Sandy's kids were adopted or she had given up a baby.

Before I could say anything, she began talking in a monotone that I barely recognized as her voice. I wasn't even sure she was talking to me. "I'm adopted, too. When I was thirteen years old, I wasn't very happy with my adoptive parents, probably the way no thirteen-year-old is." She paused, as if focused intently on the memory, not expecting me to participate in the narration. "I got it into my head that I was going to find my 'real' mother, who I guess I knew lived in a town an hour or so away when I was born. I didn't know her name or anything else, just that she had lived in this other town.

"One Saturday morning, I left home like I was going to a friend's house and got on a Greyhound bus to find my mother," she continued in that far-away voice. "When I got to her town, obviously I didn't have any idea what to do. I didn't know anything about her at all. She probably didn't even live in that town anymore. Stupid. After wandering around all day, I got on another bus and went home. My parents never even knew I did it, at least I don't think so."

It was my turn to be empathetic with a storyteller. "You weren't alone among adopted kids in wanting to find your birth parents, particularly at that age. But it doesn't sound like any harm was done. Did you try again when you were old enough to make sense of things?"

Quickly: "No! You don't understand." Her low monotone was gone, replaced by anger. "Within six months, both my parents were dead. Dad died of cancer shortly after it was discovered. Mom died in a car accident. I tried to put all of this out of my mind, but now you've brought it all back. I can't stop believing that my betrayal killed them, whether they knew it or not."

"Sandy...." I sagged in my chair. I started to say, "You can't really believe that," but it was plain that she did believe it. I stumbled through platitudes, then: "Have you ever talked to anyone, I mean, a professional, about any of this? Someone who might be able to help you work things out?"

Sandy was done with the conversation, her response abrupt. "No. I'm fine. I'm past it. Forget about it." She was dismissing me, along with the churned-up guilt.

In the years since, Sandy never asked me about the Throwaways. We talked about her latest adventures as a hot-air balloonist, our jobs, my wife, her husband and kids, mainstream topics of conversation. Other adoptees' visceral curiosity about my details has led to interesting conversations. I wasn't going to have that experience with Sandy.

My storytelling became a bridge across my austerity. I enjoyed the warmth people showed as my story unfolded, but reactions like Sandy's kept me cautious. When a new acquaintance might innocently ask whether I had any brothers and sisters, I had to decide how to answer the deceptively complicated question. There were two standard answers: The first, that I was one of seven children, would only be offered if I was ready to go farther into the story when the questioner asked more questions. The other, "No, I was raised as an only child," was used to end the discussion. The lawyer in me liked the uncooperative accuracy of the second statement—I *was* raised, if not *born*, an only child—even if it wouldn't measure up to the truth, the whole truth, and nothing but the truth.

16

"You won't believe it!" Linda skipped the niceties when I picked up the phone. "Noelle just got a letter from Ellie." Ellie, the youngest Keeper? Linda was right. I couldn't believe that one of our three missing siblings had surfaced.

Linda's tone of voice alone foretold the letter's contents. "I've never heard Noelle so excited. Sounded like she called as soon as she opened the envelope. It said Ellie and Greg had just found out about us."

Greg. My brother Greg. The original target of my search had fallen out of focus, pushed aside by the Throwaways. I smiled to myself, then realized that the young associate sitting on the other side of my desk was watching me intently. "Hold on, Linda, would you?" I held the receiver away from my face and whispered that the call might take a while. She took the hint and gathered up her files. "Sorry. I'm back."

Linda spoke breathlessly. "The letter was short but amazing, sort of like, 'We're so ashamed of what our parents did and so sorry we have missed having you as part of our lives.'" It was hard to square my excitement with the concepts of shame and sorrow. Linda's voice matched my emotions as she kept chattering. "Ellie must have found Noelle's address somewhere in her Mom's stuff after Sarah gave her one of those passive-aggressive hints about us, so she used the only thing she could find to reach us."

"Fantastic." I said it quietly, already running through the possibilities in my mind. I hadn't allowed questions about the Keepers to distract me until now. Absorbing my three sisters and their families had been enough over the last few months, but Sarah's children had been a blank spot that my curiosity needed to fill.

Linda's voice was thick with irony. "They asked if we had any interest in meeting them. It's really sad, like they think we might have something against them."

I shook my head, if only to myself. "After all the time we've spent talking about whether they know we exist, what they're all about, whether they think we're trouble, here they come at us with the same questions. What did Noelle do?"

"Aside from having a cow, nothing. She called me. Why don't you check in with her and get her to read you the letter?"

"Fine, but is there any question that we're going to…?"

Linda spoke confidently. "Not for me."

⋆ ⋆ ⋆

Ellie's handwritten letter to Noelle was just a page long, its second paragraph the most remarkable: "Seeing your smiling faces," apparently in photographs of the Throwaways' first meeting that Linda had sent to Sarah, "took my breath away—so many emotions all at once. Shame over what Mom and Dad did, anger, but mostly grief, I think, over what could have been."

Barely a week after Noelle received that first letter from the Keepers, all of the Throwaways were at my house, waiting nervously for Ellie and Greg to arrive. By then we all had spent hours on the phone with each other, reminiscent of those first calls among the Throwaways five months before. All, that is, but Mary, the seventh sibling, who icily refused to join in her brother and sister's overtures to us. The rest of us had ignored the challenges that made it hard to get together so soon; kids' schedules were juggled with spouses and neighbors, money was found for plane tickets.

I called Ellie the night before her three-hour drive north to D.C.

She lived a few minutes away from her parents, who were not aware of their daughter's travel plans. "Hey, little sister." I was no longer the youngest of the group. "Any more progress with getting Mary to join in?" Mary lived less than an hour away from Tibby and me and would have been a five-minute detour from Greg and Ellie's route to our house.

"To tell you the truth, I haven't tried again today. I already know her answer."

"I don't get it. Why wouldn't she want to be part of this?" Part of *me*. I tried not to take it as a slap.

"It's complicated. She's angry at everybody. Mom and Dad because of what they did. Greg and me for wanting to get to know you. Dawn and Noelle for confronting her all those years ago." Ellie was holding back, choosing her words carefully, not ready to tell me everything. I didn't know whether she was protecting her sister, her parents, or me.

"At least I didn't hear my name on the list. Would she let me talk to her?" I wanted to take control of the situation. It just wasn't possible that she wouldn't want to meet us.

Ellie exhaled dismissively. "Not a chance. Lord knows what that might do to her. I think you'd better accept that she's not going to change her mind, at least not soon. Sorry, but you weren't on the list only because you just fall into the general category of 'those people.'" She mimicked her sister's disgust when she said "those people."

"You're saying it wouldn't take much to make me more than just an un-indicted co-conspirator."

"I think that phone call you had in mind would be enough. We need to leave her alone for now. And I've had it with her accusations."

"Accusations?" Anger was rising in my voice.

"Forget it. We can talk about that some other time." Ellie laughed self-consciously. "You'll know soon enough what sort of family you avoided being a part of."

In all those calls over the past few days, we had stayed away from the most intrusive questions about life in Sarah and Dan Jones's house. It seemed to be an unstated rule of engagement that some things just weren't ripe for discussion. So, instead of nudging at Ellie's remark, I went back to pestering her about what had and hadn't been done to convince her sister to bring attendance at the first meeting of the Keepers and Throwaways to a hundred percent.

She sighed. "David. I promise to try one more time before we leave. But she isn't going to come with us. Trust me."

"Okay, okay. I got it." Was I more disappointed because I thought Mary was going to miss out on a remarkable moment in our lives or because my need for completeness was going to be denied? Six-of-seven felt nothing like seven-of-seven to me. I needed to shake myself from the sense of failure that was already forming in the back of my mind.

✳ ✳ ✳

Linda brought her video camera for the occasion; we propped it on the fireplace mantle in the living room, aimed at the front door. She wanted to capture every one of our first minutes together with the Keepers. The camera also recorded the last few minutes of our nervous wait as the girls peered out the front windows, watching a car turn into our cul-de-sac and Greg and Ellie walking toward the door. A childless couple has little need for a video camera, no baby's first steps to preserve. Videotape had become an unexpected diary for Tibby and me.

We couldn't resist a lame joke. The Keepers were greeted, at the end of their long drive, by a sign taped to the brass doorknocker:

MIKE AND ELLIE:
SORRY, SOMETHING CAME UP.

COULD WE GET TOGETHER NEXT WEEKEND?
BEST REGARDS,
YOUR BROTHER AND SISTERS

Greg banged loudly on the door: "You can't get rid of us that easy!"
Tibby opened the door to our newest brother and sister. I hung back,
wanting to watch events happen in front of me for a few seconds. I
realized later that my perspective had been close to that of the video
camera, certainly literally and maybe figuratively. I had stood just
beside the camera, out of its frame. I don't know whether I was trying
to be an efficient observer of a remarkable event or was once again
protecting myself from something that could expose my emotions to
the unknown.

Greg slowly and silently hugged each of his new sisters. Looking
back, it would be as quiet as I would know him to be. He is a salesman,
in all senses of the word. I would learn that his normal entry into a
new room was a noisy event; he tried to capture a crowd whether or
not it wanted to be captured. But he was subdued by the occasion, the
new territory we had all entered.

Greg gave me a very firm handshake, his rough-skinned hand
seeming to swallow mine, and pulled me to him for a hug. He was an
inch or two shorter, but felt big. He was burlier, with a long angular
face like mine and the same black hair, though with a bit more gray in
it. In that first embrace, I could tell he was a cigarette smoker.

If it would take a while for me to admit that Greg and I were oppo-
sites in many ways, it was quickly apparent that he and Ellie had little
in common. Their contrasts would become almost comically stark. If
Greg was likely to be talking, Ellie was as likely to be listening. While I
could see that Greg and I had our father's features, at least those I could
make out from the few un-posed pictures Linda had shown me, Ellie's
face looked more like the young Sarah in Linda's photo collection.

She's the tallest of the sisters. Until meeting her new sisters, she always thought she was five-feet-ten-inches tall. But standing among three other women who all proclaimed themselves at least five-ten, Ellie later confessed that she went home that night and, putting tape measure to the newly etched mark on her bedroom doorframe, found herself to be a full six feet tall.

Ellie, I soon realized, is a creative woman with a spiritual streak. At the time, she was an art curator at a well-known historical museum and a hobbyist in a range of artistic media. All of my sisters seemed to have gotten the creative gene that I lacked. Hearing them compare notes on their artistic and musical pastimes, I felt like the homeless guy looking through the plate-glass window at the diners in an expense-account restaurant.

We took dozens of pictures, recorded a mile of videotape, and passed around albums of photographs of the Throwaways' childhoods and earlier reunions. Greg and Ellie had not brought similar evidence of their family's history; it didn't seem like an oversight in planning for their trip. You could see that they were struggling with loyalty to their parents and sister. Sarah and Dan would have been as opposed to the reunion as Mary was, if they knew about it. I didn't need to ask Greg or Ellie what their parents' views might be. Our birth parents wanted secrecy.

* * *

We had been sitting around a long table in our family room, the remnants of lunch in front of us. Greg pulled a pack of cigarettes from his shirt pocket. "Mind if I head out to your patio for a quick smoke?"

"Course not," I said. "I'll keep you company." Then, as I held the screen door open for him: "So I have a silly question for you, Greg." I smiled, signaling that it really would be a silly question, not one of the difficult ones about life with our birth parents.

"Shoot," he said with a curious look.

"You ever been on the D.C. subway on a weekday morning, say from out in the Virginia suburbs heading into downtown?" Greg and I looked like brothers, but not enough for him to have been the Metro-riding twin that Tibby's co-worker had seen. I figured it was time to put that myth aside.

"Can't say I have. Why?" He lit a cigarette and puffed deeply.

I told Greg the story, how it had shaken me into getting on with the search for him. "So I'm grateful to a guy I guess I'll never meet. The image of you, maybe walking down the street in front of my office, was too much to ignore."

My brother stared silently at me for a few seconds, flicked his spent cigarette onto the grass, then nodded. "Good thing that guy was on the subway that day. I'm real happy to be here." He smiled, then clapped his hands. "But enough of that. Let's talk about something important. You play golf?"

I laughed and, as if an echo, we heard more laughter through the open door, our cue to rejoin the party. "Back inside?" I asked, nodding toward the house. Following Greg through the door, I thought of the only sibling who wasn't here, and cautiously raised the subject. "You didn't have the chance to stop by Mary's house on the way up?"

My four sisters and Tibby had been talking loudly as they began to clear dishes from the table just inside the door. Conversation ended abruptly, replaced by silent interest in the answer to the question that I hadn't wanted to become the center of attention. Mary's absence had seemed out of bounds, just as questions about the Keepers' childhoods had, but my disappointment overrode concern for damaging the buoyant atmosphere in the room.

Greg looked uncomfortably at Ellie, then back at me. "We didn't bother. No point."

I pushed. "Too bad. I don't know what she's got on her mind, but I have to believe she would have gotten something good out of this."

Greg seemed to want to say more, but resisted. "I'm sure she would have. Maybe next time." He looked at Ellie again, as if asking to be taken out of the spotlight for once.

She took the hint. "Mary has some things she has to work through. Having her here probably wouldn't have been good for any of us yet."

Greg was suddenly less sympathetic. "Hey, I got some things to work through, too. Like the fact that I was the only one of the three of us who never heard a word—not even those weird clues you say Mom tossed at you girls over the years—that any of this was going on." He took a quick breath and continued at a higher pitch. "At least y'all knew that these guys existed, that they'd been talking to Mom for years. How am I supposed to feel about that? I'm the oldest son, and I'm treated like a baby." Greg was hurt. None of us had an answer for him.

Tibby stood next to me, a plate of leftovers in her hand, a frown on her face. "I'm sorry your parents treated you that way, Greg. It's not fair. And that makes it easier for me to see how Mary might feel, too." She turned to Ellie with a sympathetic look on her face, as if apologizing for what she was about to say. "It sounds like she grew up as best she could in a messed-up family. Now she's married and has two kids of her own. Maybe all she wants is stability."

Tibby scanned all of our faces, looking for understanding. "Meeting all of you has been wonderful for David and me, but it has been…." She wasn't sure what word to use.

Linda jumped in, laughing. "A nightmare?"

Tibby smiled, but remained serious. "No, not a nightmare for us. But if Mary is worried about protecting her family, this could all feel scary, disruptive."

I looked at Tibby, nodding slightly. Our organized existence had been disrupted. We had built a life that had become too orderly even to add a dog to the mix. We loved dogs, but had a long list of reasons why we shouldn't let one complicate our plans. Now we were developing intense relationships with people we hadn't expected would be part of our lives.

Tibby seemed almost protective of the sister we hadn't met, and I realized that my wife had a right to a different perspective than mine. Of all the pictures that were shot that day, Tibby was absent from most because she was behind the camera taking them. For all of the food and wine, she was the chef and wine steward. She had been the wife of an only child, leading an organized life. Had I made her just an interested bystander to events that would affect her world?

* * *

I wanted to get some kind of childhood impressions from Ellie, even if life in the Jones household was a delicate subject. I caught her standing alone in the living room, leaning in to take a closer look at one of my favorite paintings.

"That's one of the first realistic paintings we bought." It was a large architectural oil with side views of two warehouses fronting a narrow street running away from the viewer toward a desolate waterfront in the background. "I think the bold colors and strict geometry the artist used to create the facades acted as a subconscious bridge to the abstract paintings we liked in the past." I wanted to sound knowledgeable to my art curator sister.

"It's interesting how those strong colors blend together visually to form an image that seems so subdued, calm." She moved to a picture on the next wall, standing in the classic museum-goer pose, arms crossed and leaning back from the hips.

I followed her, unconsciously adopting the same pose. "Were you into art as a kid?" It seemed like a good starting place on the topic of interest to me.

She spoke without turning from the picture. "A lot of my play time revolved around one art project or another."

"Friends?" I hoped that my tone signaled only casual interest.

"Sure, but mostly at school. We didn't bring a lot of kids over to the house."

"Oh?" I tried to make it an indirect invitation for her to keep going.

"Mom and Dad both worked by then. Did you know Mom was even a school-bus driver?"

"Nope."

"We sure were embarrassed by that. What kids want their mom to be a school-bus driver? At least she didn't drive the buses that we took to school."

I smiled, nodding my head at my own memories. "I know what you mean. My mom was a school teacher. She even taught at my junior high school for a while, or I eventually became a student at the school where she taught. I made sure that our paths *never* crossed during the school day, and she was a good sport about it. Of course, I was only too happy to ride home from school in her car, rather than take the bus, at least so long as the other kids didn't see me. Ah, to be thirteen again!" The thought wasn't appealing.

"I'd never go back, thank you." Ellie paused, unsure whether she wanted to say what was on her mind. "Things were always so...so tense. I was under strict orders always to come straight home from school, let myself in, and wait for Mom to finish her bus route."

"That's not so bad. I probably had the same orders when Mom wasn't at home."

"But I'll bet you weren't told *never* to answer the door bell or pick up the phone when you were home alone." Ellie stared at me.

My answer came out involuntarily as a whisper: "No, I can't say I was."

Her voice became as soft. "Years later, after I figured out that y'all existed, Mom was angry with me about something I'd said about the whole mess. Almost out of the blue, she said, 'See? That's why you weren't allowed to answer the door. It might have been one of *them*.'"

One of us.

17

" I don't think I said 'thank you' for all of your hard work this weekend, Petunia," I said, too casually, as I stared at the road in front of me. We were driving back from our last airport run, dropping Noelle off for her flight back to Jacksonville.

Tibby was silent, looking out the car window at the Potomac River and the Lincoln Memorial off in the distance as we drove toward Memorial Bridge. The river was brown from heavy rains that had hit West Virginia before the weekend; rainfall that far upriver took a few days to flow through Washington. I honked the horn at a car in the right lane that seemed intent on occupying the same space as ours. Tibby glowered at the driver as we sped past. "Butt-head," she sputtered.

I cut my eyes over to her. "Busy weekend, huh? Tibby's eyes stayed focused on the scenery, her head still turned away from me.

"You okay, pal?" I poked her in the side.

She pulled away. "Just tired." Her voice was thin.

"You know I love you more than anything, don't you?"

"*Si, mi amor*. I just need a break—and a nap."

Tibby wasn't used to sharing me, and I wasn't used to being shared. I needed to learn how to stay the husband she knew while incorporating the Keepers and the rest of the Throwaways into our lives.

* * *

Three days after meeting Ellie and Greg in Washington, I invited myself to a convention that one of my law partners was attending in

Ellie's hometown. I disappeared from the opening day's events soon after arriving and met Ellie for a walk through the historic district of the town where she worked. We crunched along the gravel pathways past the restored Colonial-era buildings. I impulsively grabbed her hand, caught up in the emotions of being with my sister in her world.

It wasn't my style to hold hands in public, and I sensed that it wasn't Ellie's either as soon as I took her hand. We walked along for a half-block before letting our hands drop away. Our destination was the imposing museum where her latest art installation was on exhibit.

Ellie stopped and looked around as we turned toward the main doors. "Um...there's a chance we'll run into some of my colleagues while we're in the building."

"Okay." I wasn't getting the point.

"They don't know anything about y'all." Us. The Throwaways.

"Oh. Yeah." My face reddened; I had put my sister in an awkward situation. This was all a lot easier for the Throwaways than for the Keepers. The Throwaways wanted to tell everyone our story, but we had to respect that Ellie and Greg were still living in a secretive world imposed on them by their parents. "We don't have to go in. Sorry. I hadn't thought about the spot it might put you in."

"No, no. I want you to see what I do." Ellie looked cautiously toward the museum's entrance as she spoke. "It's just, well, we *do* look a lot alike."

I made a face. "I'm not *that* homely."

Ignoring me: "What do you say to being my out-of-town cousin? The only problem is some of my co-workers know my parents pretty well." Sarah and Dan Jones lived a mile from where we stood. "Lord help me if someone mentions to Mom that I was showing around 'my cousin.'"

"Why don't I just take your lead if we run into someone?"

She nodded, looking edgily through the plate-glass doors of the museum. "One more thing." With a guilty grin: "Would you mind if we take a side stairwell up to the third floor?"

I laughed. "Don't worry. It won't be the first time someone tried to hide me from view. I seem to have that effect on people."

As we tromped up the stairs, the door to the second floor popped open and two women began down toward us. "Hi, Ellie. Coming back from an early lunch?"

I froze, waiting for Ellie to signal the approach. "No, just showing a friend around the museum." Turning to me, "Darlene, this is David from Washington, D.C. He and his wife are art buffs I met on one of my trips up to the Smithsonian." We exchanged quick hellos while Ellie continued purposefully up the stairs.

As we left the stairwell on the third floor, I looked over at my sister with eyebrows raised. She shook her head and sighed. "Probably the worst candidate for that meeting," she explained. "Darlene's family used to be our neighbors when we were growing up. They lived next door to the house where Mom and Dad still are. Thank God she didn't say anything about us looking alike. I wouldn't have been able to use the cousin thing with her. It might have gotten back to Mom."

"Sorry." I seemed to be saying that a lot.

"Not your fault." Ellie pointed to a doorway just down the hall. "Here's the exhibit."

Ellie's expertise in eighteenth-century art extended to the portraits of Charles Willson Peale and his contemporaries. She seemed to relax into the role of curator lecturing on the collection of paintings by Peale and artists he influenced. Her down-to-earth insights into the dated style of the works drew me in.

Ellie interrupted her lecture, as if suddenly remembering her unusual audience. "One of Peale's relatives, a grand-niece I think, painted the best likeness of the governor." Her eyes wandered absently around the walls of the exhibition room, looking for a painting that wasn't there. "We don't own any of her works. She lived and worked long after the museum's period of interest."

"You mean *our* governor, the legendary great-great-great grand-daddy Henry Wise?" We had talked about the governor two days before in D.C. Greg and Ellie had confirmed the fables of our lineage back to the eccentric Southern politician. They stressed the importance of his legacy to their mother. I hadn't told them that the governor had been a safe diversion in the ambivalent search for my birth family.

"That's the one, although I never remember how many 'greats' there are in there. Sarah Miriam Peale was the artist. It's hanging in the Virginia Museum in Richmond, at least it was the last time I was there. I just read that it's going to be part of a traveling exhibit of paintings by Charles Willson Peale and his family—at the Corcoran in Washington this summer. We'll all have to go see it."

"*All* of us?" I asked with a laugh.

"No, smarty-pants. Mom, Dad, and Mary would probably send their regrets." The thought of her parents brought Ellie back to the vulnerability of the moment. She looked around cautiously. "I guess we better go." Down the stairs and out a side door. Ellie had kept her secret intact, but I didn't like feeling the need to skulk around. Secrets had kept me away from the truth for too long. Could I make my birth family see that it was time to reveal their past?

* * *

Ellie and Greg had been vague about life with their parents. But at Christmas, two months after we first met, Ellie sent each Throwaway a little ring-bound album with a note: "Although Mom allowed us to copy these photos, she's not entirely comfortable with the idea. She's still very opposed to any personal contact, fearing that 'people will find out.'" I flipped slowly through the pictures, studying the images of Dan and Sarah as children, young adults, and parents, seeing hints of Greg and Ellie, but not of me.

In one picture my birth father and three-year-old sister Mary, the missing Keeper, stood alone in silhouette, backs to the camera, against the backdrop of a lake. Dan held the tiny girl's up-stretched hand in his right hand, his left in his pocket. The photograph was taken from twenty feet away, with Dan squarely centered in the frame, Mary off to the right side, the left half of the photograph empty but for the background scenery. I smiled at the whimsical idea that the photographer (my birth mother Sarah?) had subconsciously left room in the frame for me. I would have been barely a year older than Mary. What had happened during that year to put Mary in the frame and keep me out of it?

* * *

Ellie's typed note at the bottom of the picture said that it was taken on the campus of the University of Richmond. I would have been living sixty miles away while my adoptive father pursued his degree at the University of Virginia. Or I might have been at my grandparents' house on the opposite side of Richmond, playing in their big garden under the watchful eye of my maternal grandmother, the matriarch of the family. Her interest in the story of the Keepers and Throwaways would have been intense, but she had died a half dozen years before I began to learn the truth of my birth family.

As my grandmother's long life was drawing to an end, the family assembled to ensure that she did not die alone in her hospital bed. I was in my mid-thirties by then, and had come from Washington to help my mother through a hard time. I was dozing late at night on a folding cot the nurses set up in the hospital room, once they realized that someone from the family would be there to the end.

Grandmother drifted in and out of thin consciousness, her

communications limited to soft whimpers. In response to one of her sad noises after midnight, I roused myself and sat on the edge of her bed, holding her hand but receiving no response to my touch.

The door pushed open, throwing dim light across my grand-mother's bed. I had expected one of the nurses on rounds, but saw my cousin Joe. He was a few months younger than I was and, although we had grown up eight hundred miles apart, we had been together as kids in Richmond for most summers. We had known each other well, and liked each other despite our differences. Joe was the athlete; I was the scholar. He was a little shorter, but had the lean, muscular physique, the perfect symmetry, of heroic Greek statuary. There didn't seem to be a sport or physical game that he couldn't quickly master, frustrating me whenever we competed in the backyard.

My cousin's arrival shook me out of my haze. I slid off the side of Grandmother's bed, happy to see him even under these circumstances. "Joe! I didn't know you were in town."

"Yeah, man. I came over from Newport News to see Grandmother. How's she doing?" He cast his eyes past me in the darkened room to the outline of a woman we both loved.

"Not so good. They say it's time. I don't think she knows I'm here."

Joe moved over to the side of the bed and bent down. Softly: "Hi, Grandmother. It's Joe. How are you?" He spoke with the distinctive Richmond accent I had never been around long enough to absorb; "hi" had come out "haa."

"I don't think she can hear…." Her eyes opened.

"Joe? Is that you, Joe?" Grandmother's voice was a reedy whisper.

"Yes, Grandmother. I'm here. I'm so happy to see you."

"Are you doing all right, honey?" Her voice became stronger.

"Yes. Everything's just fine." Fahn.

"Are you sure?" Her words were those of the grandmother Joe and I both remembered as kids, the one who fixed her kind but crisp stare on you when she wanted the real answer. Now her eyes barely seemed to focus, her voice a faint scratch, but the effect was the same.

"Promise." Joe said the word softly, almost as quietly as his grandmother had asked the question. His confidence was failing. He'd been in trouble as a young adult, trouble that still followed him, and knew that our grandmother worried about his future.

Grandmother's eyes closed and she seemed to drift off. My cousin stood by the bed, his hand on hers for a few moments, and then turned to me. "Pretty bad, huh?" He seemed unemotional. He had seen more in his life than I had in mine.

"Well, actually, Joe, that's the most she's said to anybody since I've been around. I'm...I'm kind of amazed. You seemed to fire her up."

He shrugged and looked at his watch. "I'm out of here. Mom and Dad will be waiting up for me. I came straight here. See you later?"

"Sure. I'm sticking around until things are sorted out," gesturing toward our grandmother, again a silent figure under the white sheets. "Will you be at your parents' in the morning?"

"I dunno." He stretched, his arms clasped behind his head. "Gotta get back to work before they give me grief."

We looked at each other, not sure what to say next. Joe turned and gave me a glancing hug. "See ya." He walked quickly out the door.

I sat on the edge of my cot, then lay back slowly. I stared up at the ceiling tiles, mulling over what I had just seen. My beloved grandmother didn't seem to know that I had been her companion, but a brief visit from someone who had been a worry for decades elicited an enormous effort from her deathbed. He was her flesh and blood, and I wasn't. I was instantly ashamed for cheapening the love my grandmother had shown me. But was it possible that, so close to death, left with nothing but end-of-the-day instincts, it could all be reduced to flesh and blood? I had not yet met a biological relative back then, so I lacked a frame of reference. I was left to sleep-deprived speculation beside my silent grandmother.

18

The pace we had set in creating a new family inevitably began to slow. What had seemed like constant communication between the siblings settled into a more occasional pattern, one that I assumed was beginning to imitate the normal relationships between scattered brothers and sisters.

As the new-family whirlwind abated, my relationship with Greg began to stand out as the most complicated. A seven-year age differ-ence didn't seem like much between two men in their forties, but Greg was clearly a man of another generation. His generation was that of my senior partners: guys who believed it still should be a man's world. And our personalities added to the complexity. Greg came with an un-embarrassable confidence that he could eventually win over anybody through charismatic force. After years in business, I admired from a *long* distance the seemingly innate ability of sales guys like Greg to capture the spotlight. It was becoming clear to me that we would not have occupied the same emotional or intellectual space if we'd grown up together as brothers.

Tibby picked up the phone one evening. She made a face as she pushed the phone at me, her hand over the mouthpiece. "It's your brother." She aped a whiny tone, sneering as she rocked her head from side to side. "'Is David in?' No 'Hi, Tibby. This is Greg. How are you today?' I guess I'm just your secretary." This was not the first time that Tibby had bristled at Greg's treatment of her. She was right that Greg viewed her as a bit player in his life story. I tried to pretend that it wasn't that way.

I took the phone from her, offered a sheepish grin and shrugged my shoulders. "Hello? Oh, hi, Greg. I guess Tibby didn't know it was you, since you didn't acknowledge her."

Greg ignored the jab, or maybe he just wasn't listening. "Hey, I was thinking about coming up sometime soon, maybe over the weekend, so that you and I could play a little golf. Just the two of us. Make it a guy thing, you know?" I got the point: no Tibby. At least that's how I took it at the time. Greg had played into my guilty perception that I had let Tibby be shoved aside too often in this new family, even if he was really just using his man's-world tools to build a relationship with me.

I wasn't going to yield. "Gee, Greg, I don't know. I'm on the road so much these days that the idea of disappearing on the weekend to play golf without Tibby isn't very appealing. We don't get to see enough of each other as it is."

Tibby got the sense of what Greg was suggesting. She tossed her book down on the kitchen counter and gestured with her hands as if to say, "Fine, you boys just go on off by yourselves."

Greg seemed to be mulling over the premise that I might not choose him over Tibby. "Well, I suppose we could bring her along. Where do you want to play?"

"First, I don't think this weekend works, so we'll need to check calendars for a date that's good for all three of us." I looked sideways at Tibby, knowing what her reaction would be. She wagged a finger at me, mouthing the words "not me."

I put my hand over the mouthpiece. "Come on, Poodle."

Tibby shook her head. "If he doesn't want me around, I don't need to be around."

"I don't think he meant anything by it. He's just trying to do the male-bonding thing." Tibby seemed more aggravated than I would have expected.

I had been touched by the enthusiasm Greg showed for wanting to be part of my life. He was the brother whose shadow had teased me for thirty years. But as our relationship developed over the next few months, it became harder to ignore the differences in our values and perceptions of life, differences that were becoming more sharply defined every day. I was almost a caricature of the big-city liberal, so I worked to keep from wincing when Greg loudly offered his opinions on most social issues.

I felt that it was just a matter of time before Greg and I would have to agree to some new rules of engagement, if I had the confidence to state them to him. That seems like a harsh notion now—"rules of engagement"—but I had no other sense of how to build a relationship with my brother, especially in such an abbreviated lifetime together.

If we had known each other as brothers for forty years, we would have worked out our differences in personality and politics long ago, or would have gone our distant ways. Unless we had chosen the latter course, we would have found a shorthand method of dealing with our differences, amiably pointing out how foolish the other's views were or avoiding well-marked interpersonal minefields. But in this accelerated version of the game we were playing, the rules were so much harder to understand. I didn't want to risk damaging this new relationship, whatever it was going to be—at least not yet.

✷ ✷ ✷

"Happy anniversary!" Linda shouted as soon as I answered the phone. She started to sing the "Birthday Song," modified for the event, in a silly voice: "Happy anniversary to you, happy anniversary to you…."

I tried to stop her. "Okay, okay."

Refusing to stop: "Happy anniversary, *dear younger-but-uglier-brother-whose-mother-loves-me-best.*"

"Stop. You're killing me."

"Happy – anniversary – to – *you!*" Big crescendo.

"Who *is* this?"

"Hey, little bro! Don't you wish you could roll the clock back one year and not return my phone call?" It was Mothers Day 1996, a year after Linda's first call to me.

"Only at moments like this."

"Aw, come on. You *love* my singing."

"Sounded like you were in labor," I said, with mock horror in my voice.

"Hey, I might start to get the idea you *don't* like my singing."

"And here I didn't think you were bright enough to pick up on subtleties."

"Sooo, I hope you won't mind what I did today." Linda's tone had become tentative.

"With you I'm not sure I can imagine what you *might* have done today, so the lawyer in me requires that I reserve judgment pending further inquiry."

Linda noisily took in a deep breath before speaking. "I called Sarah today to wish her a happy Mothers Day. I hadn't spoken to her for a long time, mostly because I didn't want to get a lot of garbage from her about meeting Greg and Ellie." Her voice shifted from stern to near-whimper. "I just know she's twisting inside because we have so much contact with her kids, and she doesn't have any control over it."

I countered her sympathy with cold words. "Too bad." Nothing had happened to improve my view of Sarah since those few phone calls more than a year ago, and the very narrow glimpses I had gotten of the Keepers' childhoods hadn't helped her image.

"I know, I know. But you've got to understand her. Actually, that's what I wanted to talk to you about. I think it would be good for you, and for Sarah, to meet each other. She's met me and Noelle, probably won't ever meet Dawn, but I'm still working on that. Wouldn't you like to at least *see* her? Aren't you a little curious?"

I *was* curious. "So what's the dress code for this little affair? I assume you've worked out all the other details already." My flippancy hid a fast heartbeat.

"No. I'm not that bad. I did take her temperature on *my* coming down to see her after so long. She seemed to think that would be okay. So I just kinda said, 'Oh, and maybe I'll bring David and his wife along with me, since I'll be staying with them when I come that way anyway.' How do ya like that? Now you've got me as a houseguest again."

I was listening intently. "How did she react to that idea?"

"She didn't say no. I moved away from the topic for a little while and then brought it up again, trying not to scare her off, as usual. I told her I just happened to be going to D.C. for the Memorial Day weekend." Linda laughed. "I hope you weren't planning to be out of town then, but you better be around if I can pull this off."

"It would be great to see you, no matter what. And I have to admit I'd really like to meet Sarah." My birth mother would no longer just be a troubled voice on the telephone or a murky image built on the impressions of my siblings and a few out-of-date photographs.

"Now don't get too excited," Linda cautioned. "Sarah could change her mind at any minute, right up to the time we're pulling up to her front door."

"Front door? What about her husband? I mean, dear old Dad?"

"I spoke too fast. I doubt we actually go to their house. I didn't even mention Dan, and I'm sure she didn't for a minute consider involving him in this. I think we need to enlist Ellie's help."

"Sounds right to me. How will she feel about it?" I thought my youngest Keeper sister had the right to be uneasy about exposing her parents to me, churning up the silt of a childhood that she might want left undisturbed.

"She wants you to meet your mother. I'm sure she'd like to put us all together—her father and sister included—to heal all the old wounds. Maybe more than any of the rest of us."

19

I met my birth mother for the first time in a hotel lobby. The room looked and smelled like a composite of all the other bland hotels that were a theme of my life on the road. Sanitized-for-your-protection elevator music played loudly overhead as we surveyed the generic furniture arranged in front of the fake fireplace.

We staked out a spot for the meeting, willing the tourists who walked through the lobby to keep on moving. We had ended up here because the hotel's side door was only a few hundred yards from my birth parents' house, an easy walk for Sarah, at least physically. But it had the empty feel of a neutral zone, a place to meet when the participants feel at risk. It was too late to change our plans, but this setting was only going to add to the awkwardness of meeting Sarah.

The night before, we had been planning to head south to see Sarah. But then I sat in our living room watching Linda's frustrated side of a string of phone calls with our birth mother. Sarah was losing her nerve. It was beginning to feel unlikely that I would be meeting her anytime soon.

Linda sounded like she was trying to soothe a crying baby. "Oh, you poor thing. Your diverticulitis is acting up again?" Linda made a sour face, then winked at me as she cradled the phone between her shoulder and ear. "Uh huh. Uh huh." She rubbed her forehead with both hands. "Don't worry about a thing. If you're not feeling well, we can just visit for a few minutes." More muffled words from Sarah, an anxious list of reasons to cancel our visit.

Linda's voice shifted from soothing to stern. "Sarah. It's *you* I want

David to meet. I've had such nice visits with you over the years, and I want him to have the same opportunity to get to know you. If Dan's not interested, then he doesn't have to come with you. If he wants to live in a dream world, that's fine. Why should he stop you?"

Sarah wasn't buying it. She was worried about the reaction of a husband who still denied that I existed, and maybe she just didn't want to meet me. I shook my head at my self-pity; this wasn't about whether Sarah wanted to meet me. She was fighting a half-century of fears.

Linda pushed. "Well, our plans are all made and we're on our way in the morning. Ellie will be ready to bring you over as soon as we get there. I can't wait to see you. Bye." The last word had come out as two lilting syllables. Linda was trying to soften the effect of ending the call abruptly. She stared at the phone briefly with pursed lips and turned to me. "I decided to hang up before she said 'absolutely not.'"

"Doesn't sound like it's going to work out." I was preparing myself for failure once again.

We got on the phone with Ellie, who sounded more embarrassed than sad. "Looks like now is not the right time. Mom is really upset. She told Dad about you coming down, and he is dead set against it."

Linda spoke as I remained silent, trying to keep my disappointment under control. "I'm surprised your mom got your dad involved at all."

"Probably my fault," Ellie said with sadness in her voice. "I was trying to convince her that this would be a good thing for Dad. It would give him the chance to see that everything turned out all right. Maybe he could be at peace."

Ellie sounded exhausted, unsure of how to handle such a delicate challenge. "I asked her if I could discuss it with him, but she wouldn't let me. She must have decided to do it herself, to keep me out of the way. I have no idea what she said to him. It can't be easy for either of them. Anyway, I tried. I did what I thought was best."

"We completely understand your thinking." Linda spoke softly. I was speechless, hugely frustrated that I didn't have the power to make the meeting happen, just as I hadn't been able to pull in our missing sister. I felt like a crimson-faced, squalling two-year-old after he's been told he can't have chocolate ice cream for breakfast. My birth father and sister Mary were mysteries that I needed to resolve. The evidence was mounting that I might never get to know them, or even hear their angry voices on an answering machine. I would have no hope left if I couldn't convince Sarah to meet me when we had gotten this close.

Ellie was looking for any good news. "Will you still come down? I really want to see you, and Greg is going to try to come over, too." Her voice brightened a little. "Who knows? Maybe I can get Mom to change her mind once you get here. Don't count on it. She's pretty stubborn when she makes up her mind."

I tried to sound enthusiastic. "Sure we'll come down. We can't wait to see you." True, but I also wanted to play the long odds that Sarah would rise to the occasion. We would just have to wait until we arrived in town to learn whether I'd be meeting my birth mother.

* * *

Ellie answered on the first ring when I called from the payphone in the hotel lobby. She struggled to sound calm, but her voice was strained and her words were jammed together. "I'll go over and pick up Mom, if she doesn't change her mind three times before I get there. I almost got her to agree to have you come over to the house. I think she wanted to force Dad to face things. But it's better this way." I hung up the phone and idly thumbed the pages of the worn phone directory on the ledge below.

I had tried not to expect more than a pleasant day with my wife and two sisters—and without Sarah. Now I recognized the adrenaline heartbeat and shortness of breath that made me feel like a coward in stressful situations. I knew that my voice would have shifted up by a half-octave, always a sign that I was at my limits.

I cleared my throat and spoke softly as I turned away from the payphone, willing myself to sound more like a baritone than a tenor: "Looks like too many other hotel lobbies I've been in." The words were aimed at nothing, just an excuse to test my voice without sounding too much like a half-wit rambling to myself. Tibby looked at me curiously. I shook my head slightly, a silent statement that there was nothing for her to worry about.

We were close to achieving a goal: meeting my birth mother. But I had been so caught up in the process that I hadn't really thought about what I really hoped to accomplish. What should I expect from what was likely to happen in the next few minutes? I had done it again: So driven by the need to achieve the next objective, I had failed to consider the broader consequences of reaching that summit until they had overtaken me. I was always telling clients that they needed a business plan, a thorough long-term strategy, before they could ever expect to be successful entrepreneurs. I believed that the same was true for personal decisions. We would all be better off with at least a few defined goals to measure ourselves against. Yet here I was, waiting for Sarah to walk through the door, with no clear idea of what I wanted from her or what I should expect to give her in return.

The three of us studied the historical prints and foxhunt scenes on the walls as we waited. I could see that Tibby was tense, worried about the disappointment she didn't want me to suffer. Which version of the unpredictable Sarah would we meet?

Finally—*finally*—Ellie walked slowly through the lobby doors with a fragile looking woman on her arm. Sarah looked small next to her six-foot-tall daughter, but she would have looked frail and older than her seventy-three years regardless of her escort. She wore a cream-colored silk housecoat in a Chinese style over pale pink pants. Her short hair, pure white, was carefully done in a fluffy style like that of many women her age.

Here was the woman who knew all the secrets. The woman who denied my relationship to her, threatening me with the police, and days later sought me out to admit it. The woman who withheld from me the existence of my three Throwaway sisters, knowing that they were looking for me, and then set in motion their finding me. The woman who had kept the Throwaways from the Keepers and then given her youngest daughter enough clues to find us. My birth mother wouldn't have been standing in this hotel lobby if she hadn't found the will to face the last of her forsaken children. Even without a strategic plan for this event, I knew that I wouldn't be testing her courage today by asking the hard questions I had for her.

Sarah looked bewildered as she scanned the faces of the people in the lobby. She offered a faint smile as she decided that I must be her son—and that there didn't appear to be any nosy locals that she knew in the lobby. A public place had its advantages and disadvantages if you were trying to keep secrets from the neighbors. Linda walked to her, arms outstretched to hug the woman she had seen only a few, brief times before. Sarah seemed unsure whether to accept her daughter's embrace or to step back. Linda bent down, wrapped an arm around Sarah's shoulders and pulled the old lady toward the sofas we had staked out. Sarah allowed herself to be led.

"It's so wonderful to see you, Sarah." Linda walked over and grabbed our birth mother's hand, then almost pulled Sarah toward me. "This is David, your son," she said, warmly and slowly.

The discordance of hearing myself described as Sarah's son shook me into action. "Hello. Thank you for coming." I sounded like I was meeting a new client. Sarah accepted my right hand with hers and I put my left hand on her shoulder in an effort to soften the formality of my approach. Her hand was small and thin, chilled from the spring air and from the tension of the moment.

"Why don't you sit here?" I directed my birth mother to the sofa and sat next to her. I immediately wished that I had taken the chair opposite her; I wanted to be as nearly face-to-face as possible, the better to see what was in her eyes.

Linda began a cheery commentary, trying to ease Sarah into the group. I turned slightly sideways to study the mystery beside me, and Sarah stole self-conscious glances at me as she tried to keep up with Linda's words. I was glad that I had sat to her right. The pupil in her left eye seemed fully dilated; I remembered Ellie once making a passing comment that her mother was nearly blind in one eye but hadn't known until that moment which was her good eye.

I wanted to get into the conversation but wasn't coming up with anything to say. I gestured for Tibby to hand me a mailing tube that held a large print of the Sarah Miriam Peale painting of Governor Wise, Sarah's much-admired ancestor. Ellie had helped me track down the likeness at the Virginia Museum. I uncoiled the print and held it out for Sarah. "We thought you might like a copy of Governor Wise's painting." My birth mother looked confused for a moment. I felt compelled to blurt, "You know, our ancestor."

"Oh, my. How nice." When she didn't move to take the print from me, Ellie reached for it and said she'd make sure it was nicely framed.

"We all think David looks just like Governor Wise. Don't you think so?" Linda asked. Sarah looked from the print to me and back again.

I ran my finger along the bridge of my nose and smiled at her. "I might look more like him if I hadn't broken my nose as a kid and had it fixed. I lost the bump on the bridge of my nose that we all seem to have." Ellie uncurled the print again, and I tilted my chin to mimic the formal pose the governor had struck for his portrait. I liked seeing myself as the great man's double, even if it was a stretch. I shared the eye and hair color and angular face in the painting, but wasn't sure that the similarities could be carried much farther.

Sarah perked up. "I broke my nose as a little girl, too." She laughed. "But you can see that mine didn't get fixed." She pinched the crooked ridge of her nose.

Linda slowly pulled her ever-present video camera from her bag and pointed it toward our birth mother. Sarah quickly turned her face away. "Turn that thing off," she cried.

"Oh, come on. You look so nice." Linda kept the camera trained on Sarah, who held her hand in front of her face.

Ellie spoke as if to a child. "Mom, you're being just a little stubborn, aren't you?" Sarah pulled her hand away from her face and grimaced at the camera lens with what looked to me like a mix of fear and anger. I realized later that, even including the little photo album Ellie sent her new siblings the Christmas before, I had never seen a picture of Sarah past her twenties. Was she just one of those people who don't like having their picture taken as they age, or was it all part of hiding the truth?

My birth mother proved to be a woman of dramatic physical gestures, like those of a stage actress, but almost too big for our theater that day. She would throw her hands up in the air to emphasize a point and, a moment later, tilt her chin down and cock her head to look bashfully at us. I began to think that she might be putting on a performance. Maybe that was what she needed to do to get through a painful event.

I kept up an internal dialogue as we talked, critiquing my performance as embarrassingly stiff and clumsy. This might be my only chance to impress my birth mother, and all I could come up with were platitudes and inanities. At least I had summoned up the detached presence of mind to assess my skills on such an emotional occasion. I was fumbling for what to say and do, and yet actively studying my performance at the same time. So far, the director in me was finding the actor inadequate for his part.

We moved into a loose conversation about which of the Throwaways and Keepers looked like someone else in the family. I steered clear of the "Throwaway" and "Keeper" labels; Sarah wouldn't have appreciated my irreverence. Linda said, "I've even heard that people think David and Tibby look like brother and sister. How about that?"

Sarah seemed interested in the theme, slapping her thighs with both hands. "They said the same thing about Dan and me, but I don't see it at all."

I was relieved to feel the wise-guy in me begin to surface. I turned to Sarah with a serious look on my face. "Tibby does have a similar nose and dark hair. Just so we can get past this once and for all." I put on an impish grin, hoping to signal to my audience that a joke was ahead. "She's not my sister is she? Tibby's a year older than me, and there is that three-year gap between Linda and me."

Sarah stared blankly at me, not sure at first what I was asking. Then she let out a quick laugh, throwing her hands into the air again. Looking at Tibby, she cried out: "I swear I've never seen her before in my life!" We all laughed.

Another topic came to mind. "My mother and grandmother once took me to see the capital building in Richmond. Apparently I was fascinated by all the governors' portraits."

"Oh, yes." She spoke in a solemn tone. "They're all on the first floor."

"I don't remember where they were. Mom was worried that I might recognize myself on the wall—because of Governor Wise." Sarah seemed puzzled, maybe trying to get past my references to a mother who wasn't her. "But now that I've seen his portrait, even if it was there, I doubt I would have looked at it," gesturing to the mailing tube now propped up against a table leg, "and seen myself."

"But you do look a lot like him." Sarah put on a sad face. "You had the most beautiful pink cheeks I ever saw." It was Sarah's first real comment directed at my birth, or at the subject of me as her child, for that matter. She clutched her arms to her chest, hands together under her chin, wringing a handkerchief. Her expression was hard to read. She continued speaking in a voice so low and soft that I was having a hard time hearing it over the grating background music. I was at one of the most important events of my life and I still couldn't get the bad music out of my head. After a moment's hesitation, Sarah almost whispered: "I had asked to see you at the hospital."

"That must have been very hard." I matched her tone.

"It was. You were the only one I ever asked to see."

"Really? Why me?" I looked at Linda to see if she felt short-changed by her birth mother, but she didn't react.

"I just had to. I don't know why." She continued in an even softer voice: "We had no choice but to—just be glad you didn't have to live in those times."

"What?" I wasn't sure that I heard what she was saying over the music.

Ellie interrupted, thinking that she needed to interpret for her mother. "She means there weren't a lot of choices for them back then." Turning to her mother: "The beautiful thing is, Mom, this isn't 1946, 1956, and we're all okay with this. And we want you and Dad to be, too."

Sarah answered quickly: "I never will be, dear." Her voice was cold.

I leaned closer to Sarah. "You just have to accept it. And not just us—our parents are grateful to you and your husband." I couldn't bring myself to say "our father."

Linda: "You made a lot of people happy."

Sarah laughed softly, shaking her head. "I just kept goin' on and on, didn't I?" We laughed with her, but self-consciously. She wanted to shift topics. "I don't know how I ended up with Dan. Such different personalities."

We started to talk over each other about how couples usually were better off having different personalities. Sarah wasn't interested. She rolled her head from side to side as she spoke. "I feel sorry for poor ole Dan." Linda interrupted with assurances that she shouldn't think that way, apparently knowing, after all those years of talking to Sarah, where our birth mother was going. Sarah kept on. "Well, I'm not an easy person"—turning to her daughter Ellie—"am I? Always trying to...."

Linda stuck with her. "Oh, now, you've been a good...."

"I'm not a real...I don't know what I am. And that's the bad part. When you really get to seventy-three and you don't know what you are, or where you're coming from, that's kinda bad, isn't it?" She looked around at her audience. It might have been a good starting place for a real conversation, but not today, not here.

The reunion was drawing to an end. Linda wanted to use every minute, so she steered the conversation to health issues, figuring that it was a way to pick up a few more items for our medical histories. Sarah became animated as she detailed her health problems. She began to press herself into me, sometimes patting my knee, always twisting her handkerchief. Was she less detached from me than I had thought, but trying to keep her true emotions in check?

I looked around, wondering how surprising it might have been for the tee-shirt-and-shorts tourists walking through the lobby to know what was going on in front of them. I almost had to remind myself: You're meeting your birth mother after forty-one years. What would the guy in the Detroit Hard Rock Café shirt and Redskins cap have thought about that?

Sarah's health woes, including seemingly comprehensive allergies, left her with limited food choices. And her migraine headaches were triggered by foods, as well. I looked at her with what I hoped was sympathetic awe: "Then what do you eat?"

"Nothing."

"Oh, come on. You have to eat something." She didn't look like she was suffering from malnutrition.

"I'm telling you, nothing. I can't eat. Just caffeine-free coke and soda crackers."

Ellie rolled her eyes. "Mom, I guess we'd better get you back. Dad will be waiting." We had not talked about Dan's unwillingness to participate.

Sarah turned to me one last time. "Would you like to see Dan?" My father? Of course I wanted to see him, but was that possible? Sarah looked at us with conspiracy in her eyes. "We're going to dinner tonight at Rudolfo's," apparently an Italian restaurant in the neighborhood. "The three of you," gesturing to Tibby, Linda, and me, "could sit at a table across the room and...."

"Um." I tried not to look shocked at her suggestion, then slowly shook my head. I wasn't interested in manipulating Dan into Sarah's ambush, even if he might never know that it had happened. I looked at the others and could see their discomfort. "I don't think that would be fair," I said, as mildly as I could. "Maybe someday he'll change his mind and we can meet the right way."

Sarah looked me sternly in the eye. "I don't think so, dear." I took the coldness of her tone to mean that I had blown my one chance at seeing my birth father and that she wouldn't try again. Time would prove her right.

We stood up slowly, hugged all around, and Ellie led her mother out the door. I had no reason to believe that I would ever see my birth mother again. Nor could I ever hope to hear her answers to the bigger questions that all circled around the primary theme of "why." We had engaged in superficial diplomacy, skirting those questions. Should I have been more demanding when I had the chance? Was this a lost opportunity or just an inevitable result?

A few weeks later, after all the telephone post-mortems of our visit with Sarah, Ellie called again: "I thought you might like to know that I was over to Mom and Dad's last night." Her tone was dismissive, ridiculing. "Mom hung your framed print of Governor Wise on the living room wall right over the chair Dad sits in. And guess what? She didn't tell him where she'd gotten the picture from and he didn't ask." She laughed. "I love it. There's a picture of the governor—might as well be a picture of you—staring him in the face every day."

I liked the idea that my gift—though not really my likeness— looked down on my denying birth father in the house he never bought. Mortgages require credit ratings, and credit ratings make you traceable by people you don't want to find you.

20

My adoptive and birth parents were married a few months apart in 1947. Tibby and I weren't invited to celebrate Dan and Sarah's fiftieth wedding anniversary, but they would have been welcomed at the event we hosted for Mom and Dad in Richmond's grandest old hotel. Most of my siblings attended, including Ellie and Greg. I wondered whether my parents' warm embrace of the two Keepers from the outset had exposed an unfortunate contrast with my siblings' real parents. That topic remained mostly untouched.

Mom and Dad's relatives and longtime friends at the anniversary party had closely followed the evolution of my new family. Their interest had been fueled by my mother's creative efforts to relate the story through Christmas poems and photo-collages of the new daughters, son, and dozen grandchildren. I had never before been comfortable in the role of dancing bear, performing with my siblings for the crowd, but it felt good this time. My brother and sisters' arrival in our lives, and their enthusiasm for my parents, had made Mom and Dad very happy.

I was standing on the edge of the room reciting to myself the short speech I was about to give in my parents' honor when Ellie tugged on my jacket sleeve. "You look deep in thought, bro."

"Just running through what I want to say to everybody about Mom and Dad. There's a lot I should say, but I don't want people slumping over in their chairs."

Ellie looked around at the hundred people in the room. "Sure is a different scene than my parents' fiftieth anniversary celebration, if you could call it that."

"Yeah?" I was always interested in the chance to peer into my birth parents' private lives.

"They went to Rudolfo's, their regular spot. The only difference was that they invited us to tag along. Actually, Mary was the one who got us all together. Mom and Dad might not have done anything if she hadn't pushed it." Ellie seemed embarrassed by the details. "So it was Mary and her husband, and Greg and his girlfriend Hannah—met her yet? —and little old me."

I shook my head. I hadn't met the new girlfriend yet.

Ellie smiled. "I like her. She'll be good for Greg, if he can hold onto her."

The scene at Rudolfo's held more interest for me at the moment. "And? How'd it go?" I laughed. "I mean Rudolfo's, not Greg's date."

"And it was just like you'd expect. Or at least like I would expect. They pretended that having a glass of wine was a rare thing for them. I didn't say, 'Maybe you'd prefer a bottle of vodka and two glasses.'" Ellie considered her parents to be alcoholics.

"We sat there not talking about any of the things that were on our minds—my mind, anyway. Bless his heart, Greg looked like he was getting up the nerve to confront Dad about you all one more time." Ellie shook her head slowly, a sign of resignation. "But he had a couple of drinks, too, and I think Hannah told him this wasn't the time to tackle the subject. So we sat there acting nice. It was pathetic."

"Sorry." Ellie hadn't seemed to be looking for sympathy, but I felt the need to offer it.

She flicked the wrist of one hand dismissively and looked around the room. "I'm used to it. Just appreciate what you have." We saw Greg at the same time, as he advanced on us with a cocktail glass in hand. Ellie leaned into me, whispering, "And here comes Greg. Ask him about the dinner with Mom and Dad, if you're ready for his version. Might be very different from mine."

"That's okay. I think I got the picture."

Greg looked satisfied with himself. "Well, if it isn't my baby sister and baby brother. What are you brats talking about?" He squeezed my shoulder with one big paw and faked a gut punch with the other.

I reflexively pulled back from the punch. "We were saying that we're surprised Sarah and Dan had any more kids after spawning you. Maybe they decided to keep trying until they got it right?"

"Guess that's why they kept throwing the bad ones away. Gotcha!" Greg shifted so that he was between Ellie and me, with his back to her. He lowered his voice as if to shut our sister out of the conversation. "Can we go somewhere this evening and talk? Let's smoke a cigar. I have something to discuss with you." Ellie smirked and started to walk away.

I grabbed her sleeve. "Don't leave yet. We haven't finished." We probably had finished, but I didn't want our brother to control the process. Greg thought he had been treated for most of his life without the respect he deserved. Now he was working hard to reclaim his place as the big brother.

Ellie laughed and gave us an elaborate goodbye wave. In an exaggerated, posh-English accent: "I have other loyal subjects to consider. I shall be off."

I turned back to Greg, who suddenly looked tense. My face must have reflected concern that something bad was about to happen. He laughed. "Don't worry. It's a good thing—for a change."

My initial reaction was excusable. Over the year and a half that I had known him, Greg had begun to draw me into the very personal challenges facing him with his ex-wives, children, and employers. Greg's life seemed to be in turmoil, and I had been proud that he would see me as someone whose guidance he valued. The lawyer in me had tried to help Greg rethink the nature of whatever his latest problem might be. We always came to a solution, and I got to feel good about helping out my brother. It would be several years before I understood that my suggested solution would only be his course of action if he hadn't gotten someone else's opinion by the time he confronted the antagonist at the center of that day's drama.

This time I relaxed, at least as much as I could as I prepared to get our guests' attention for the speechmaking. "Right. Let's have that cigar tonight, after Mom and Dad have quit for the night. Tibby will probably want to head up to our hotel room fairly early, too."

* * *

Greg and I sat in the courtyard of a neighborhood bar smoking the cigars someone had given him. "I didn't want to say too much during your mom and dad's party. Didn't want to take away from their big moment, but Hannah and I want to announce that we've decided to get married."

"Great news." I did think it was great news.

Greg looked me in the eye. "I'd like you to be my best man." My face flushed with the happy surprise I felt. I had never been anybody's best man before, much less for a brother I had only known for eighteen months.

"Greg, I'm flattered. And I'm delighted to accept. Now I just have to guess what a best man is supposed to do." The idea of my being someone's best man had never occurred to me before; there wouldn't have been anyone I thought might *want* me to be his best man.

"Don't worry about it, big guy. You know I'm always happy to tell you what to do." He laughed.

I began to think more clearly. "But isn't there a problem with me being your best man?"

"Like what?"

"Well, how do you think your parents would feel about attending a wedding with me standing there with you? Do you think that might just be an issue for them?"

"Hannah and I talked about that. We decided we were going to ask everyone we cared about to attend the wedding. You, Tibby, your parents, *all* of my sisters— including Mary," that distant Keeper who still refused to join the fun, "and Mom and Dad. Everybody can decide for themselves whether they want to attend. If someone doesn't want to be there, too bad."

"I don't want to cause…."

"Look, David, I'm not sure my parents would even attend the wedding anyway. And Mary doesn't approve of much of my life, either. You and the girls, and your parents, are the best family I've got. You've all been wonderful to Hannah. She and I want you all at the wedding." Greg sighed. "I hope Mom and Dad will be there, too, but I'm not counting on it. Okay?" The last word was spoken in the tone of a challenge.

I held my hands out in surrender and spoke meekly. "Okay." I decided that, for once, I didn't have any grounds to question Greg's reasoning.

"We're going to get married one year from today, on your parents' next anniversary. We couldn't think of a better inspiration than their wedding day for the beginning of our marriage."

*　*　*

One year minus one day later, I stood next to a golf cart on a course in Greg's hometown. As Greg's friends began to arrive for a golfing bachelor's party the day before his third wedding, I was self-consciously trying to act like one of the guys. I knew that I could give the impression of an elitist, coat-and-tie lawyer, so I was working hard at not standing out in this crowd. Sometimes working hard at not doing something is a recipe for disaster, but disaster quickly seemed likely no matter how I acted.

Greg had stocked several of the ten golf carts with quart bottles of bourbon. The bottles would be empty, along with many six-packs of beer, long before we reached the eighteenth hole. The rangers on the course quickly identified me as the soberest member of the group and demanded that I somehow corral our errant carts back in the general direction of the holes we were supposed to be playing. Wanting only to fit in, I instead found myself playing the role of the schoolmarm in the detention hall. I was a relative newcomer to golf and tried to play within its many rules of decorum, so the rangers' glares stung me. I should have shrugged my shoulders and laughed, giving in to my brother's ambitions for the day, but that never occurred to me.

I hung onto the windshield frame as Greg weaved our cart across what was beginning to feel like an endless string of fairways. I had lost the energy to respond to his barbs about how bad my game was. He might have thought it was all in the nature of big brother/little brother competition, but I was beginning to feel under siege from every direction. Golf is a game of concentration, something I had a hard time bringing to the sport under the best of circumstances. These were not the best of circumstances, and I was overly self-conscious about my lack of skill at the game. If I had taken a moment to look at the mayhem around me, I would have seen that none of Greg's friends cared how *anyone* was playing, least of all me.

The gods did not seem to be smiling down on me as I stood on the next tee studying a par-three hole with a terrifying pond in front of the green. I took a practice swing and addressed the ball. Greg kept up a running monologue with our playing partners on his shot the last time he had played this hole.

"...and the wind was coming in hard from the right so I basically aimed at the tree-line maybe twenty yards over there. See where that tall tree is? Right about there. And..."

I turned away from the ball and interrupted him. "Greg, I'm trying to hit and you're not making it any easier."

"Sorry, big guy." Greg turned and shrugged at the other players, flicking his cigarette butt to the ground and mashing it with his heel.

I swung, surprising myself at the relatively clean shot. Greg provided the play-by-play: "Hey, not bad." He sounded shocked. "A little high." He was squinting into the sun, one hand blocking the glare. "Don't think it's gonna make it. Good line, though."

The ball splashed into the pond, ten yards short of the green. I sighed. Greg pulled a ball from his golf bag, then tossed it onto the ground at my feet. "Tee it up again. Won't count, but you need the practice."

I slowly bent down and teed up the ball. I would have refused, but thought it might be satisfying to put one of his golf balls into the pond.

"Keep your head down." Greg stood behind me, checking my posture. "Take the club back slow. Keep your eye on the ball."

I swung the club back quickly and brought it down at the ball as hard as I could. Speed and force usually cause bad results for beginning golfers, but that was my goal this time. A random sequence of events conspired instead to carry my ball over the pond and onto the right collar of the green. I couldn't decide whether to enjoy watching the ball roll onto dry land or to curse the failure of my secret plan.

Greg stood silently for a moment, then: "That shot was better than your first."

I could feel my face flush as I turned to him, sputtering: "You think? Brilliant deduction, Sherlock." I slammed my club back into the bag on the back of the cart and slung myself onto the seat. Greg opened his mouth to come back at me, then reconsidered. He lit a cigarette, slowly slid behind the wheel of the cart, and sighed deeply as we took off for the next hole.

I was a lawyer who prided himself on staying cool, above the fray, in difficult situations. I was quick to tell clients not to be distracted by petty emotions that might obscure the right decision. I realized, as I bumped along the golf course with my brother, that I was letting a silly situation—one that should have encouraged teasing laughter rather than steam—get the better of me. But the realization wasn't enough to shake me out of my childishness.

Greg was just trying to have fun with his buddies, including me. That should have been enough for me, to spend the day the way he wanted. After so short a tenure with my siblings, was I already developing the sensitivities, the hair-trigger rising out of old familial grievances, that other siblings my age have taken a lifetime to develop? Or maybe it was simpler than that: Maybe I was just an indulged, only child now being forced to find my way, not entirely successfully, in a world where I didn't get to set the rules anymore.

* * *

Tibby laughed as I described the day's entertainment for her. I had convinced her to take golf lessons with me when clients pressured me into trying the game. She had been my principal golf partner since then, and we rarely traveled on vacations without dragging our clubs along. This time, though, in the weeks before the wedding, Greg had made it pointedly clear that women weren't invited to his golf outing. This was another guy thing, so mine were the only set of clubs in the trunk of our car as we headed down the road for the wedding.

"It's such a shame that I had to miss the fun." Tibby had a perky smile on her face, pretending to mask her sarcasm.

I grimaced. "Oh, well. The sad life of a golf widow. At least we didn't end up in a strip club." I couldn't imagine that scene.

"But you would have gone along if they insisted, wouldn't you?" Tibby knew that those kinds of places embarrassed me. I had watched clients make fools of themselves in front of dancing women who clearly weren't interested in anything but the men's wallets.

"No I wouldn't." I tried to sound confident in response, but I wasn't sure that I was telling the truth.

Tibby looked at me as if she knew I wasn't telling the truth. "Do you know how to say 'no' to any of this?"

I guess I didn't. And I couldn't voice my guilt about how petty I had been with Greg that afternoon. Tibby would have assured me that I was dead right with my emotions, but I wasn't so sure. Greg could be challenging sometimes, but maybe I was too judgmental in return.

* * *

My sister Linda had flown to D.C. to spend a night with us before we drove down to Virginia Beach for Greg and Hannah's wedding. Mom and Dad, Dawn, Noelle, and her husband were all coming for the wedding. Ellie would attend her brother's wedding, but her sister Mary and their parents would not. The presence of the Throwaways doomed any prospect that our birth parents and missing sibling might participate, but Greg had held out hope for a grand reconciliation around his wedding.

"How did the guest list shape up?" I asked while Greg and I were huddled over last minute details in the hotel bar. It was another one of those dark-wood-and-cigarette-smoke places, with multiple TVs tuned to CNN and ESPN with the volume muted. I usually found myself drawn to the closed-captioning scrawl along the bottoms of the screens, with the misspellings and hopeless guesses by the typists as to what the fast-talking commentators were actually saying. It became an impromptu video game to figure out what the fractured messages meant.

Greg shrugged his shoulders and rolled his head, as if releasing tension in his neck. "Molly's supposed to be here, but it's prom night so there seem to be a lot of complications from that." His teenaged daughter was injecting high-school drama into the event.

"How about Mike?" Greg's oldest child, a college student.

Greg blew out a thin stream of cigarette smoke, shaking his head slowly. "Don't think so. Haven't heard a word from him since I left a message with his roommate two weeks ago."

"What did your parents have to say?" I hadn't raised the issue in the weeks before the wedding.

"What do you think? Mom acted as if I was just asking them out to dinner. 'I don't think we will be able to make it, dear.'" He shrugged his shoulders.

"Sorry, guy. But I guess that was to be expected." Greg looked straight ahead at his reflection in the mirror behind the bar, saying nothing. I nudged his shoulder with mine. "Right?" He nodded, tipped his head back, and blew another stream of smoke up toward the ceiling.

* * *

"Check this out." Greg had come up to me in the hallway outside the hotel meeting room where the wedding would take place. He turned away and bent his left leg back at the knee to show me the sole of his shoe. I looked down and saw that he had written the word "help" in block letters on it. He duplicated the process to show the word "me" printed on the sole of his right shoe.

"Isn't that going to be great when we kneel down in front of the preacher to pray? Funny, huh?" Greg could see on my face that I was about to question his wisdom. "Aw, come on, David. It's just a wedding."

As the ceremony was concluding, I stood off to my brother's right facing the forty people in the audience from my best-man station. The minister asked the newly married couple to kneel before him for the final prayer. Greg winked at me as he dropped to his knees and seemed to point the bottoms of his shoes slightly upward to attract attention to them.

I scanned the faces of the audience, most of whom had by now bowed their heads. I looked down at Greg and self-consciously nodded my head, acknowledging the joke that no one else in the room seemed to notice. Greg was having a good time and I should have been happy for him. But his idea of a good time and mine were very different. Why couldn't I just accept that?

A half-hour later I was reviewing the toast I was about to give in a tightly packed, upstairs banquet room of the hotel. I had labored to make my first toast as a best man a good one.

Greg rushed over to me, his tie missing and collar button undone: "The cigars! What about the cigars?"

"What cigars?" I asked in sudden panic.

"You mean there aren't any after-dinner cigars?"

I had failed to meet the minimum standards for a best man. I hadn't thought about cigars. It never occurred to me to give him a so-sorry look and say that we would just have to do without them. I raced over to Tibby: "Pip, I gotta go out for a few minutes."

"What? Now? Dinner is about to be served."

"I know." I looked at my watch. "But it's close to six o'clock and I'm not sure any decent place to get cigars will be open by the time we get through dinner."

"What's so important about cigars?"

I looked over toward my brother. "Well, Greg...."

"If he wanted them he should have gotten them himself." Tibby struggled to keep her voice down, looking around to make sure no one was listening.

"But I'm the best man. I won't be gone long." Within minutes I had left the hotel after grabbing a puzzled bellhop and demanding to know where the closest cigar shop might be. It was only as I jumped back in the car after leaving the store I had miraculously stumbled across that

I stopped to reflect on what an idiot I was. Would I have been as malleable with a brother I had known forever, or would I have been quick to tell him to buzz off after a lifetime of perceived and actual assaults?

* * *

On an unexpectedly warm fall day, Tibby and I wilted into the painful wooden benches of the little, un-air-conditioned chapel on the grounds of Washington's National Cathedral. Our pew felt as if it wanted to pitch us unceremoniously forward into the aisle, rejecting us as unholy. Maybe that's the Episcopalian way.

I had no duties at this wedding, other than to acknowledge to the usher that we belonged on the bride's side of the church. I didn't know the groom, soon to be our neighbors' son-in-law; Tibby reminded me that we had met him in passing months before. But I could see, without looking at the wedding program, that the best man at his side before the altar was an older brother. The groom still looked like what he was, a guy between college and business school. His stylishly unruly hair had been tempered for the occasion. The best-man brother looked at least a few years older.

I focused on the two men throughout the ceremony. They reminded me of what I had wanted when I began looking for my brother: someone enough like me to have shared and refined the experiences of life. I understood then that mine had been a foolish enterprise from the start.

Even if my brother had been the perfect embodiment of my hopes for him, he and I would never be brothers whose lives had been shared from the beginning. I left the chapel knowing that I could let myself be a different brother to my siblings, the brother who had come sideways into their lives just moments before. I inhaled deeply as we escaped the stiff air of the church.

21

I began to feel a sense of urgency, a need to write down the details of my altered existence before the memories faded. I wasn't interested in keeping an informal journal; I needed structure, a beginning, a middle, and an end, not the random anecdotes that a diary seemed to invite.

I wanted to tell a complete story. It couldn't just be about discovering the Keepers and Throwaways, meeting my birth mother, and learning to be part of a different kind of family. I was a lawyer, trained to seek all of the facts and analyze them carefully. How could I write the story without knowing the answer to the most important question: Why? Why had Sarah and Dan Jones had a string of children and given them up for adoption? It was the question that everyone who heard the story eventually asked. The gaping hole in my knowledge became a barrier.

Most lawyers think they are good writers. Many are, at least in the technical sense; their nouns and verb tenses usually agree. I enjoyed writing, even if it was only to produce another legal memorandum. The act of writing helped me see things more clearly, opened my mind to connections that weren't apparent beforehand. I was rarely more focused than while trying to get the right words on paper.

I was sure that, if I could just get started, I would see things more clearly in writing. Maybe I'd even make progress on the "why" question. Writing a memoir would take time, and creativity that I wasn't sure I had, but I slowly convinced myself that it would be worth the effort in the end. I was part of a good story and wanted to be the one to tell it.

I decided that fiction was the answer. If I didn't know why my birth parents had done what they did, then I would take the few facts I had at the time, at least the blurred memories that had become facts in the minds of the Keepers, and weave them into a fictional account of my birth parents' early lives. That gimmick gave me the freedom to fill in the gaps, to build for my birth parents a fictional existence that explained what they did.

It never occurred to me that I was forcing the future, that I had no business pretending to write a "complete" story when it wasn't close to finished yet. I had known the Keepers and Throwaways for barely two years and had met Sarah just the year before. The only story I had to tell at the time was the first-person chronology of an adoptee finding some of his birth family. But I persisted; I had defined an objective and, as usual, would pursue it without amendment.

I loved writing the fiction for the freedom it offered. I thought my fiction flowed while the pure autobiography was stiff on the page. A chapter of fact was followed, almost as a reward, by a chapter of fantasy wrapped around skimpy facts.

It began like this: Dan and Sarah were married shortly after World War II and promptly had a son whose medical problems were a financial and emotional strain on them. Their marriage and the birth of my brother are undeniable, but I imagined that Greg's medical issues were just a convenient excuse reported in the Throwaways' adoption files.

My fiction picked up from there and fleshed out a marriage that was strained from the beginning, fueled by Dan's frustrated physical abuse of his son and sexual abuse of his wife, Sarah's severe mood swings, and their mutual alcoholism. The life I began to build for my birth parents was ugly, and Dan seemed to bear the brunt of my stories. He refused to acknowledge my existence, so I made his unappealing.

* * *

My stories were not all aimed at debasing my birth parents. I created what I thought were entertaining characters to fill out the supporting roles, like the adoption attorney who placed the first two Throwaways with the same family against Sarah's wishes. I tried to make the fictional Dan and Sarah interesting, but I couldn't spin their lives into happy ones.

I had told my sisters that I was trying to write about my experiences. Completing the first draft of a manuscript meant that I would finally have to decide whether to show it to any of them. I created aliases for my siblings and birth parents, pretending that doing so would soften the intrusion. I tried not to borrow any of my siblings' personal stories, because those were theirs to tell.

I called Ellie. "I think I'm finally done with the piece I've been writing." I was wrong about that. I had barely begun; the fiction would over time fade into irrelevance.

"The one about us? When do I get to read it?" I had wanted her to ask that question, but now wasn't so sure. She was going to be my test case, the sensitive artist with a calloused view of her parents.

"Maybe never. It's just something I felt like I needed to do."

"Oh." She sounded disappointed. "Okay. But I'd really be interested."

"Thanks. We'll see." I thought the manuscript was pretty good and wanted others to share that opinion. "I'm not sure you would want to read it."

"Why's that?"

"Some of what I wrote is pretty harsh. I don't paint a very pretty picture of your parents, or at least what I imagined about them." I let out an embarrassed laugh. "Maybe I'm not sure how *I* would feel about you reading it."

Ellie snorted. "David." Pause. "There's nothing you could have written that's harsher than the truth of how we lived."

* * *

I was relieved when I saw the subject line on Ellie's email: "The best manuscript I've read this year," followed by the first line of text: "OK, it's the ONLY manuscript I've read this year...." It was a good sign; she could joke about my fictionalization of her parents' lives.

Ellie wrote in her email that our "story when told on the screen should be a comedy. I see a riotous scene in which the Throwaways have just met Mom all together for the first time, and seeing what lies ahead on the biological road, convene back at their hotel to frantically compare notes on good psychiatrists they've used, the women dumping their purses to compare drug prescriptions." I had shown the manuscript to a few friends, but Ellie's was the first reaction from someone other than Tibby who had lived what I was writing.

Her long email was rich with personal details. "I was also surprised to hear you describe your early anxiety over school and it triggered memories of mine at the same age. I thought it was due to the tension at home, but maybe that's something in our psyche? I too was good at schoolwork, so why be afraid? It was the social skills I lacked. Or so I thought. Perhaps it was a chemical imbalance/panic attack/anxiety disorder. Fear of being perfect?"

My manuscript had reminded her, and now she was reminding me, of childhood terrors. Ellie is seven years younger than me, the same age gap that I have with Greg. I doubt that I would have been any better at mentoring her through her fears than my older brother would have been with me.

And my manuscript brought out deeper insights into her parents: "As for the descriptions of Dad that you were so worried about me reading...well, one can't imagine one's own parents having sex...and I especially can't imagine Dad as a rapist. It's as good a theory as any, but Dad as sicko pervert didn't ring true. Mom never spared telling me inappropriate things, so if he'd been a brute in bed she would've held that against him, too, and verbalized it." My face would have reddened with embarrassment as I saw those words, remembering just how rough I had portrayed the sexual relationship to be. Why had I ever considered that part of my writings appropriate to show Ellie?

But she seemed to have taken it in stride: "I think underneath it all, he was really a very sensitive soul, but that scared him and he blunted the fear with booze and withdrew. I thought he had been the force behind giving away all of those babies, but I now wonder, is that because he'd seen the depths of HER despair and knew she wasn't a fit mother?"

Ellie still wanted to soften the image that she was creating: "I think Greg and I haven't done a very good job of telling the Throwaways the good things about them."

I had gotten used to the idea that Dan and Sarah were nightmarish parents, but was still interested in reading something positive. I was the product of these people and carried some of them with me; I didn't want to worry about which of their flaws were ingrained in me without hoping that a few good characteristics were thrown into the mix as well.

Ellie's words gave me shallow comfort: "They were dimensional people. Just paralyzed emotionally. But I couldn't help remembering the times he took us kite flying, or fishing, or to teach us how to hit tennis balls. Or to play putt-putt. It's just that those memories got overshadowed by the shame of him being sent home bombed from the driving range bar where he'd scrawled something obscene on a napkin for the cocktail waitress. Or some other episode."

My sister wrote that Sarah was "harder to describe. Even the good times with her seemed underscored by resentment, or her lack of self-esteem would kill the joy in any situation." I skimmed Ellie's recollections of her mother, but was drawn back to the paragraphs about her father. At least I had some contact with Sarah, some independent knowledge of her, but I was again forced to rely solely on someone else to understand Dan Jones. And this time in a medium that didn't even give me a voice on the other end of a telephone line to study for nuances.

The more I learned about my birth father, the more I realized that I couldn't be confident about the picture I was drawing of him in my mind. I still hung onto remote hope that Dan Jones would come out of hiding one day so that I could judge him for myself, but time was running out.

22

E llie wanted my legal advice on how to deal with her father's declining health and rising medical expenses. "I feel kind of odd asking for your help on all of this, and you can just say 'no' if it feels too weird." Her voice was tentative over the phone.

"Why wouldn't I want to?"

Ellie adopted a jokingly sarcastic tone: "Could it have anything to do with the fact that I'm asking you to help me with the man who still refuses to admit that you are his child? And to do it behind the scenes, without Dad—or Mary—knowing about it? Just maybe?" It stung more that her sister needed to be coddled. I had accepted what I saw as my birth father's cowardice, but couldn't accept Mary's cold rejection of the Throwaways.

"Forget about it. If it makes you feel any better, I have to admit I get perverse satisfaction out of helping him. Maybe I'll send him a bill for my time." I was helping my sister, not my birth father. It was late summer 2002. I had known Ellie for seven years.

Dan Jones was in the hospital for what turned out to be the last time. Meanwhile, Sarah had fallen while home alone and ended up in a different hospital.

"She was drunk when she fell, of course." Ellie's acid carried clearly over the phone line. "As soon as we knew that she was going to be all right, Greg and I went over to the house and started looking for their stash."

"Stash?"

"Vodka. We found bottles hidden all over the place—broom

closet, behind the firewood out back, in the baby crib Mom keeps in her bedroom. We guess they hid bottles from each other and then forgot where they were."

"From each other?"

"Yep," she said confidently. "I think they tried to pretend—even to each other—that they weren't alcoholics." She paused, but I remained silent, unsure of what to say. "See what we've been dealing with all of these years? Still happy to be part of the family?"

"We don't get to choose parents. At least I didn't have to live with them." Not the right thing to say to a sister who had lived with them. "Sorry. That was stupid."

"It's nothing I haven't thought about myself. You *didn't* have to live with them. And I'm sorry to drag you into this now. But you might as well know what's going on." Ellie had tried to get her mother into a detox program at the hospital, but Sarah had refused. "They can't make her do it, I guess. Now they're going to transfer her to a nursing home for physical therapy. I'm hoping the nursing home can get her some kind of psychiatric evaluation while she's there."

"Any chance?" I had learned that the law made it hard to get help for people who didn't want it.

"I'm doing as much advance politicking as I can. I sat down and typed up a timeline of all the dysfunctional things I could remember she had done over the years. That was a sickening trip down memory lane. But maybe it will convince them of what I suspect."

"Which is?"

Ellie paused to organize her thoughts, I guessed, then spoke crisply. "I've been doing a lot of research on bi-polar disorder, manic depression. She's got all the symptoms. In fact, reading about it, I'm stunned that nobody checked her out for this a long time ago."

I myself had only the most *Popular Science* understanding of the bi-polar disorder, a general sense of the frenzied highs with their periods of great, but ill-focused, activity followed by the bleakest depression, a cycle destined to be repeated for a lifetime in the absence of serious medication and counseling. It seemed like a tough illness to beat, partly because its victims were often smarter than average and able to convince themselves that they didn't really have a problem that needed to be solved.

I thought about my first, hot-and-cold telephone calls with Sarah, back when she was either screaming at me or passively confused as to who I was. I decided to leave those memories unspoken for now. "Interesting. If you're right, maybe she's been able to hide the symptoms as well as she hid all those pregnancies." Good thing Tibby and I didn't have any kids. My DNA was looking ragged.

"She may have hidden them from everybody else, but Dad and the three of us kids sure saw the symptoms."

"What's on this timeline of yours?" I asked cautiously. It sounded like something I could have used when I wrote my fiction about Sarah, but then I would have been more hemmed in by facts.

"You want me to send it to you? I hate to pile this stuff on you, but a lot of it you've already heard, I think. I probably never did describe for you how our house would be filthy for months and then she would go on a tear and force us to help clean the whole place, top to bottom, in one day. This was back in the early 1970s, so I was ten or so."

I could hear Ellie flipping through the pages of her notes, apparently deciding which episodes to share with me. "In retrospect,' she continued, "I'd say she was drinking heavily then, too, but that may just be hindsight. The shoplifting is a clear memory, though. More than once I saw her steal all of the silverware and fixtures from restaurant tables, just to see if she could. It was like she wanted the danger. And bad checks all the time."

"Send the timeline if you get a chance." I wanted to change the subject. I no longer had any idealized notions of my birth parents, but

I felt my own merit being diminished every time another of Dan and Sarah Jones's failings was revealed.

Ellie spoke in a distracted voice, more to herself than to me. "I'm just looking through what I've already written down. This copy of my timeline is so marked up with things I forgot to put in the first time. It's a mess, literally and figuratively." Then, in a put-on happy voice: "Oh, yes. And, of course, there's the train story."

"The train story?"

"I must have told you that one."

"Don't think so."

"That's one I'm sure you'd remember if I had."

"Let's hear it then, I suppose."

Ellie inhaled deeply, as if stocking up air for a deep dive into the pool. "When I was about five years old, I was riding in the back seat of a two-door car. Like a Thunderbird or Mustang. You know?"

"Sure."

"Mom was in the passenger seat and one of her equally crazy girl-friends was driving. We were going over a railroad track when the car stalled. Off in the distance we could see a train coming. Mom and her friend opened the car doors and jumped out. I started to push the front seat forward so I could get out. Mom reached into the car, put her hand on the seat, and pushed it back towards me. She looked at me and said," Ellie's voice becoming soft and sing-song, "'No, dear. You stay in the car.'"

Impossible, I thought. Too evil to be possible. "Unbelievable," I said. A variation on "impossible" that could convey something other than denial. "What happened?"

"Well, obviously I'm here to tell the story. The train managed to stop inches away from the car. The engineer jumped out screaming at Mom and her friend, and I guess at that point Mom knew that she could be in big trouble if the engineer saw I was left in the car, so she opened the door and pulled me out before the guy noticed."

"I don't know what to say."

My sister laughed; at least it sounded like a laugh. "I always knew I was on my own. Mom and Dad didn't really pay a lot of attention to me. I don't remember what, if anything, happened after that. I'm sure Mom went on like nothing did. She probably was sorry I didn't die in a train wreck. Then she could really have done the poor-little-me martyrdom thing and been rid of me on top of it. Of course, she and her friend probably were drunk at the time, so maybe I shouldn't hold her too accountable. I don't know."

Ellie anticipated what I was thinking. "The funny thing is, I mentioned this to Mary after we started getting along again, probably because I wasn't so sure my memory was real. She told me that she remembered Mom making a joke out of it at the time."

"A joke—like 'Oh, by the way, I forgot your little sister in the backseat of a car that was about to get hit by a train, silly me?'"

"I don't know. She might have been afraid I would say something to Mary and wanted to derail it. Pardon the pun. But I feel more confident that it happened, since Mary remembered something about it."

Whether or not "the train story" happened, my sister had a childhood in which she thought it could have happened.

23

I was being thrown from side to side, constrained only by my
seat belt, in the back seat of a car forcing its way down crowded
California Highway 101 in the late afternoon. Two business
partners and I were hurrying from the Sonoma Valley to the Oakland
airport to catch flights. I had escaped the law-firm life a few years
before and now found myself in less predictable places, chasing after
opportunities to make a difference and a living at the same time.

I was destined for the red-eye on a discount carrier back to D.C.
I didn't care; I just wanted to get home. No one seemed to mind that
the driver was aggressively slaloming our rental car through traffic,
weaving so close to the bumpers of the cars we passed that I was convinced we had actually nicked one of them a few miles back.

My cell phone rang. I had turned sideways and stretched my legs
across the width of the seat, my feet pressed up against the armrest
of the opposite door to keep me from shifting constantly with the
swerving of our car. I dug clumsily into a pants pocket for the phone
while trying to keep my balance on the seat. The phone's screen said
it was Tibby calling. I looked at my watch. Six p.m. here meant nine
p.m. in D.C., Tibby's preferred bedtime, and I had failed to call her
earlier.

"Sorry, Pip. Time got away from me. Are you in your jammies?"
Her early-to-bed-early-to-rise routine was a regular subject of my
teasing.

"Not yet. Where are you?"

"Sitting in the back seat of a bumper car being driven by crazy

Jerry." I shifted to keep from sliding off the seat as Jerry pumped the brakes hard to avoid the delivery truck that had foolishly pulled in front of our semi-guided missile. I leaned forward and flicked him on the side of the head. "Dammit, Jerry. I'd rather get there late than not at all!"

Tibby would ordinarily have quizzed me about what was going on, but not this time. "Greg left a message on our answering machine this afternoon."

"Greg Thomas?" Another business partner at the time.

"No, Greg Jones." She didn't say it with the edge in her voice that I would have expected. Something was up.

"What did he have to say?" It could have been anything with him.

"It was convoluted, but…. He said Dan died this morning."

I stared out the window at the oddly barren, rolling hills speeding past. I wasn't sure what I had to say about the news. He wasn't my father, at least not beyond a biological contribution. I had never met him. And that was my first reaction: I never met the man.

"You there?" The cell phone was still stuck to my ear, momentarily forgotten.

"Yeah. Sorry."

"No problem. Just thought the call might have been dropped." Tibby spoke quietly, wanting to gauge my reaction to the news without pressing me.

I bought time for processing my thoughts. "How did Greg sound? Should I call him?"

"I guess so. He sounded okay, not too upset. Said they were busy making funeral arrangements and dealing with Sarah. I think he said she's still in the nursing home."

*   *   *

As we passed San Quentin prison and drove across one of the long
bay bridges into Oakland, I called my sister Linda to give her the news.
She would have seen my cell phone number pop up on caller ID and
answered with a cheery "Hey there."

"Hey. Listen," I said quietly, not really wanting my car mates' attention to turn to this conversation with Linda. "Tibby just called to tell
me that we got a message from Greg. Dan died."

She responded quickly, as if his death was just a dry fact. "Guessed
I'd hear that sometime soon." She sounded the way I thought I had
when Tibby told me the news, her voice betraying little obvious
emotion. Then: "Little brother, you seem so sad." Her tone was too
soothing. She assumed that I was upset by Dan's death, but I don't
think I had put much more inflection into our brief conversation than
she had. Was she as unsure of her feelings as I had been, reacting by
assigning an emotion to me that was as much hers?

"Not so much sad. Maybe disappointed. I'd like to have had the
chance to help him set things right. Now that won't happen."

"It would never have happened."

"Probably right, but …."

"I know. David, I feel so sorry for you."

"Why should you?" I felt like she was putting words to thoughts I
didn't have. "I didn't know the guy any more than you did."

"But I gave up any expectations a long time ago. I don't think you
did. After all, you've been part of this for a lot shorter time than me.
I guess after that one time Sarah threw me in front of him under false
pretenses, I just put him behind me."

I swiveled around on the car seat, dropping my legs back to the
floor and sitting up straight, at least until my head grazed the low
roofline. "You know what it is? I'm angry at the guy. He's dead and I'm
angry. He had answers. And he probably wasn't as poor an excuse for
a human as I imagine. I'd like to have had the chance to figure that out

for myself. Maybe he would have been an even *bigger* waste of space than I thought. Who knows? But now I can't get there."

"You never would have. It wasn't going to happen."

"Maybe."

"Listen to me: It – would – never – happen. Period."

"Maybe." I should have tried harder to get to him. I was a lawyer, a persuader. Now I couldn't hope to understand my birth father. He had escaped.

* * *

I didn't see Dan's obituary, posted on the Web by the local paper, until late on the day he was buried. The notice said that a "private service" was held two days after he died. His newspaper tombstone described him as survived by his wife, three children, four grandchildren, and a sister. Truth and fiction in one simple declaration.

I asked Ellie who had attended. "It was a sad affair. Just Mom, Greg and his latest girlfriend, Mary and her husband, and me." Greg's girlfriend was the successor to Hannah, who was soon to become an ex-wife. My services as best man had not helped to save my brother's third marriage from the fate of the others.

"I noticed it was a 'private service.'"

Pause. "Mary wanted it that way. She was afraid one of you all might show up." One of us Throwaways. Not only was the missing Keeper avoiding us, she was assigning intentions to people she didn't know.

"Right. I was thinking about wearing Groucho glasses and standing behind one of the flower arrangements. Then, at the appropriate time, I could have thrown myself on the casket, weeping hysterically." I had wondered whether I would attend Sarah's funeral one day, but I had never considered showing up for Dan's.

"That would have been *very* nice. Did you know that Dan's twin sister Marge refused to come to the funeral?"

"Greg said he called to let her know Dan died." My birth father had apparently rejected his sister's offers to visit for several years. "Greg told me she said something like, 'If he didn't want to see me in life, he wouldn't want to see me in death.'"

"Seems like we're a family that's good at holding grudges, doesn't it?" Ellie asked. "Or at least stubborn. Mom's as hard to move as Dad was."

"So how is your mother dealing with all of this?" I asked, expecting the worst. Ellie hadn't mentioned much about Sarah's participation in the funeral. She had spent the last few weeks of her husband's life in a nursing home still recovering from the fall she'd taken in Dan's absence.

"Not bad. I had no idea what to expect, but always have to anticipate the worst," parroting my thoughts. "We took her straight out of the nursing home for the funeral, so she hadn't had anything to drink. That helped. She's been at home since day before yesterday, so I suspect she's managed to get hold of alcohol through one of her old drinking buddies. I hope the detox program sticks with her, but yesterday's events don't leave me very optimistic."

"Yesterday's events?"

"Another self-inflicted crisis. Mom refuses to have any home-health aides in the house. So Greg and his girlfriend decide to spend the weekend with her, I guess thinking that they could make her more comfortable. Obviously, though, she doesn't want anyone in the house who could catch her drinking. Yesterday morning, while Greg and his girlfriend are trying to fix her breakfast, Mom calls the cops to report intruders in the house. Greg doesn't know anything about it until the police show up." Ellie spoke with fatalistic amusement.

"Perfect," I said drily. "Then?"

"Greg plus girlfriend have to go out and sit in the backyard while the cops sort things out. It doesn't take long for them to get the idea, but they tell Greg that Mom has the right to keep him out of the house if she wants to. So Greg leaves after Mom refuses to come to the door."

"What was Greg's take on all of this? He must have been pretty upset."

"Sure. He was hurt—and angry. After a while he was mostly angry. We spent our whole lives being manipulated by Mom, and we've seen much worse than this before, but we never seem to learn how to keep from being drawn in."

"We're all suckers for family gamesmanship, I guess. It's just that your parents played rougher than some."

Ellie sighed. "After all you've been through with us, I still feel strange talking to you about this stuff."

"Come on." I tried to sound dismissive, but it was awkward for me, too. I had to balance empathy for the Keepers, dismay over the darkness of my birth parents' lives, and a growing sense of powerlessness to make things better.

Ellie wasn't going to let me minimize her concern. "Seriously. This is embarrassing to talk about," she insisted. "On top of that, they're your parents, too. You might not have been raised by them, but they're in there somewhere."

She paused, as if trying to find her words. "I'm making you hear things you might be happier not knowing."

I wasn't going to tell her that I'd had precisely that thought before. "Little sister, I'm a big boy. More information is always better than less. I appreciate what you're saying, though. Believe me: It will always be less personal to me than it is to you. I'm not looking to dredge up your painful memories, but if I don't get the story from you, I'll just have to keep writing my goofy fiction. No telling what I might have them doing if you give me enough time and blank paper. Maybe a three-volume collector's edition of bad behavior by the time I'm through."

Ellie seemed to laugh out of obligation, but I hadn't lightened her mood. "It's hard to explain, but I still feel, I don't know, disloyal when I talk about Mom and Dad this way. They lived in fear of their secrets getting out. Now...."

It was time to say something that had been developing in my mind for a while: "When I started writing about all of this, I wanted to explain everything. I might not have been able to say why they decided to give up four kids for adoption, but I could try to guess why they were so secretive. The importance of the blue-blood lineage thing to your mother, Governor Wise, that kind of stuff. It wasn't all that deep an analysis, mostly pop psychology."

I hesitated, wondering whether I should keep going with my theories, but continued on. "I wanted to think that the strain of having all of us Throwaways was what turned your family life upside-down. But learning what I have has forced me to see things differently. The Throwaways weren't the cause; we were just a consequence. My ego tried to put us at the center of the story, but we weren't even close."

I could hear Ellie breathing over the phone into a long silence. Then she laughed: "That would certainly absolve you of all responsibility, wouldn't it?"

"Why else would I come up with the theory? I'm a lawyer. It's always somebody else's fault."

24

Ellie came to Washington on a quick trip for a seminar. Our schedules had seemed so mutually exclusive that we fell by default into afternoon tea at one of the city's posh downtown hotels. I had never had "tea" before, a concept that seemed more pompous than entertaining. Tibby arrived from her office a few blocks away just as my cab pulled up to the front door of the Mayflower Hotel. She pushed her cheek up for me to kiss; I always got an unhappy look from her when I failed to kiss her on first meeting.

"You look frazzled," I said as I bent down to nuzzle her cheek.

"Not the best day for this at work, but…." She squinted up at me. "You look a bit shell-shocked yourself."

"Silly board meeting took two hours in the middle of the day, and the deal closing is still jamming itself into tomorrow. It's going to be a late night." I wanted to see Ellie, but another time would have been better.

We walked arm-in-arm through the long, marbled lobby that stretches the length of the building, from Connecticut Avenue to Seventeenth Street. "Where do they serve tea, anyway?" I hadn't been in this hotel for years.

"Looks like over there." Tibby pointed to a room with spacious tables clad in white, a dozen waiters also in white—white suits, ties, and gloves—hovering over the few guests. It all looked a bit foolish to me.

Ellie had arrived first. She drew herself up in the chair, posing regally. I leaned down to give her a quick hug. Lowering her head and looking furtively around: "I'm glad I'm wearing clean underpants today."

"Hey, don't look at me. This is all Tibby's doing. She's got this thing for scones with lemon curd." I pulled the chair out for Tibby, something I rarely managed to do anymore, but it seemed necessary in this place. Mom would have been happy. I move compulsively to the outside of a sidewalk whenever I walk with a woman, one of many childhood lessons from my mother.

We talked about art, Ellie's new house, anything but the events following her father's death four months earlier. Three waiters danced around the table, wheeling a heavy silver tea service beside us and offering china platters of finger sandwiches and pastries. There were even those scones with a pot of lemon curd. I twitched my eyebrows at Ellie as I pointed to the lemon curd and said to the waiter: "Excuse me, sir, but it looks like that cream has gone bad." Tibby winced; she knew that I liked to banter with the waiters.

The waiter looked at me and followed my stare to the pot of lemon curd. In a lofty air, he said: "Oh, monsieur, that is not cream. It is a wonderful accompaniment for the scones." He pointed to the rock-hard biscuits as if he were adding those to my empty bank of knowledge as well.

"Oh, thank you very much, sir! Is it good on these little sandwiches, too?" I pointed at the white-toast wedges with salmon mousse.

Tibby hissed quietly in Spanish: "*Basta.*" Enough.

* * *

The topics we hadn't touched hung over us. It was time to address them. "Your mom doing any better?" I said it in the casual tone of "How's the weather?"

"To be honest, I try not to be able to answer that question more than once a week, which is when I check in with Angie, the lady who sits with Mom during the day. I know it sounds terrible, but that's the way I have to handle things right now. She's just too poisonous for me."

"You don't need to justify yourself to me. Whatever you think is best *is* best as far as I'm concerned."

"Thanks." Ellie sounded relieved not to have to spend any more time explaining herself. I wondered whether Greg and Mary were nagging her about seeing Sarah, but left the question unasked. "The last few times I talked with Mom, I felt like I was back in my childhood, a place I'd rather not be. I worried that at any minute she could go into one of her rages. Calm and sweet one minute…." Ellie stopped abruptly, poured more hot water into her cup, and dipped the tea bag, seeming to collect her thoughts or deciding whether to change direction. "My childhood was marked by her angry outbursts, usually including bizarre revelations. I learned a lot from those things, like that you guys existed. It almost felt like a physical assault—her torrent of words—though it never was physical. I guess it was all a part of the bi-polar disorder."

Tibby looked wide-eyed at Ellie and spoke: "Isn't it amazing that she remained undiagnosed for all those years? Maybe she could have been helped."

Ellie nodded. "Mom's a survivor, that's for sure. I guess we all were, living in that house."

"Her screaming fits could be useful?" I asked, not wanting the conversation to drift away. "Sounds like she let things slip, intentionally or otherwise, from time to time."

"I guess. But you never knew what was true and what wasn't. Like the rape." I turned my head toward her in surprise. Ellie looked down at the plate in front of her, and spoke more softly. I wasn't sure whether she was displaying embarrassment or resignation. "I don't think I ever told you about that."

"No." Another train story? I shook my head at the waiter and said "no thanks" to his offer of more hot water for my tea. I hated hot drinks, coffee or tea, under any circumstances; they made me sweat more than I already did. I wished the waiters would go away. They had become a distraction. We were at this table for reasons other than the tea and grand atmosphere.

Ellie nodded slowly. "This one's hard to figure out, and it leads to so many other questions. I was a freshman in college, still living at home. I wanted to go to some Saturday-night party in the freshman dorm, and Mom wasn't happy about the idea. She was always worried about me walking around campus after dark. Finally, she calmed down after I promised to call her when I got safely to the dorm. Of course, I forgot about my promise the minute I saw my friends. I honestly can't remember whether I really forgot or was just being defiant."

I couldn't guess where the story was going. "So I assume your mother went wild?"

"Of course. She started calling everyone she could think of. The campus police. She tried to track down the Dean of Students. Somehow she got hold of the numbers for the hall phones in the dorm—called every one of them screaming for someone to find her daughter. By the time they did, it seemed like everybody in the building knew my crazy mother was looking for me. Like any self-respecting teenager, I was humiliated. I slunk out of the dorm as fast as I could and went home."

"A happy homecoming? The prodigal daughter returns?"

"Sure. Mom tore into me. All kinds of irrational yelling. And then she starts to tell me about what happened to her at VMI."

* * *

Sarah was still in high school when she went to work as a secretary in the mathematics department at the local college. It was there that

Sarah said she had been raped. I couldn't resist fictionalizing the story when I got to that part of the manuscript the first time around.

I wrote that she was already struggling with the imbalances that would develop into manic depression within a few years. But beneath the self-doubt and mental clouds that more and more frequently controlled her thoughts, Sarah had a real quickness of mind, a cleverness that would help her to survive the years to come.

I wove together a story of her terrifying encounter as she walked home from work across the dark campus. She had been experiencing a heightened sensory state, something she had begun to feel more frequently over the past year. It signaled a lightness, a breathless excitement, unlike any she had experienced before. She liked herself better when she was riding one of these new waves of enthusiasm. If only she could evade the black times that followed.

The emotional apexes were no time for caution; they were times to do, not to think. Looking back on the violence of that night, her confused instinct was that she had done something wrong, that she had somehow caused the drunken student to assault her, but she was the one who had been violated.

* * *

I had filled in the details, pretending that I had the vision to give life to events whose specifics I would never know. It was a trivialization that embarrasses me now, but it was my strained effort to give my birth mother a context that might begin to explain the childhoods of the Keepers and the reasons for the Throwaways.

Ellie didn't know the details of the assault. "With Mom, it's always impossible to know up from down. She was so filled with drama when she told me she had been raped, but was it just drama for drama's sake, to make me feel sorry for being such a bad daughter—and to make me feel sorry for her at the same time? I was too shocked to ask lots of questions and I never talked to her about it after that. I'm sure I sound hard-hearted, but even at that age I had learned not to trust her."

"Do you really think she was capable of making up something like that just to prove a point?" I still hadn't fully grasped how frightening a mother Sarah must have been.

"Absolutely. But I'm not saying the rape didn't happen. I just can't bring myself to look at it without a healthy dose of skepticism. And I haven't told you the rest of it."

"Let me guess. Pregnant?"

"Mom got even more jumbled on that one, but she left me with the impression she did get pregnant. And what happened after that...?" Ellie shrugged her shoulders and gave us a sly smile.

"Come on. An older, *eighth* sibling? Or, I guess, *half*-sibling?"

"Well, she didn't abort the four of *you*." Ellie laughed; it was the resigned laugh of experience.

* * *

I had built the continuation of the young Sarah's story in my mind, and then on paper. I brought the story to what I saw as a clever, creative end in my manuscript. But I would learn soon enough that my fiction was a hollow vanity. So I decided to leave it behind.

25

S arah was waiting for us, leaning on a cane just inside the glass outer door of her house with the front door wide open behind her. Her blousy purple housedress looked inadequate against the cold of the winter's first snow, shortly after New Year's Day 2004. I hoped that she hadn't been standing there for very long. We should have called during the drive down from Washington to let her know when to expect us, but I couldn't give her the chance to say she no longer wanted Linda, Tibby, and me to visit. Her past mood swings couldn't be ignored, even if she hadn't given any sign that she might reject our visit. This would be the first time we had seen Sarah since that awkward meeting in the hotel lobby nearly eight years earlier.

A lot had happened in those eight years, and the most significant event for Sarah, the death of her husband and co-conspirator, had left her adrift. She needed someone to care about her, even if it meant facing the Throwaways again. I had been surprised to hear her voice on my answering machine, one night before the Christmas holidays, saying that she was just thinking about me. Listening to her recorded voice, with its happy tone, took me back to the threats she had yelled into the machine after I first contacted her. I was ready to accept a willing Sarah, but caution still seemed justified.

We crunched across the thin layer of icy snow on Sarah's front yard, my guarded optimism in tow. The simple facade of the red-brick rambler felt familiar to me; we had driven by it several times during earlier trips. The first pass had been a stealthy drive-by with Ellie at the wheel. Back then I had instructions to duck down if either of my birth parents was in the front yard.

Sarah pushed the glass door open and tested the slippery surface of the top step with her cane. Linda yelled to her cheerily: "You get back in that house. We don't want you falling and breaking your neck." Sarah waved to us like a happy little girl, a shy grin on her face. She seemed relieved to retreat behind the door.

I followed Linda and Tibby into the house, kicking snow off my shoes. I had never seen the inside of the house before, so I looked around quickly as Linda hugged Sarah. The living room was to the right, its furniture formal, with an air of grandeur in the brocade upholstery and wing chairs. What seemed to be the master bedroom was to the left. I stopped to look more carefully through its doorway after my eyes skimmed over a large baby crib at the foot of the bed.

I turned my attention back to my birth mother as she pulled away from Linda. I bent down to hug her. She looked smaller and frailer than I anticipated, an impression heightened by her hunched stance over a cane. Her white hair was carefully put together; I guessed that she had made a special trip to the beauty parlor for us.

I straightened and put my hand on Sarah's shoulder, looking back to smile at her. "It's so good to see you after all this time. Thank you for inviting the three of us to visit." I wasn't sure whether we had been invited or just allowed. The next few minutes would tell us what sort of afternoon we were going to have with Sarah. We had expected to stay for an hour or two at best, but weren't sure that her hospitality would last that long.

"Oh, no." Sarah pulled herself up with pride. "I thank you for coming. Let's go back to the sunroom." She pointed toward a door through which I could see a narrow kitchen. "We can go this way."

* * *

The night before our visit with Sarah, the three of us had discussed what we wanted to get out of the trip. It wasn't enough just to see our birth mother; we had tasks to complete. This might be the last chance to get face-to-face answers out of her, and it didn't seem to me that we were going down there because of any emotional need for another reunion. I felt sorry for Sarah and thought we were doing a good thing by visiting her, but there was no sentimentality mixed in with my objectives.

"You *know* what *I* want." Linda spoke with force in her voice. "Darn." She slapped the dinner table. "I meant to get hold of a medical-history form from some place. I want to go down the list of every ailment and find out what she had, what Dan had, what their parents had. I'm tired of guessing what my kids inherited."

"Easy enough. Let's see what's on the Internet." I gestured for Linda to follow me into my home office. I sat down and tapped on the computer keyboard. "The first one's from the Mayo Clinic." I scrolled through the document with Linda over my shoulder. "Looks good. What do you think?" My printer was already spitting out the two-pager.

"Great. There's everything you can imagine on it. And look at that one." She laughed as she tapped the screen.

"Which one? Arthritis?"

She pulled the first page from the printer. "Nope. This one." Her finger pointed to the line labeled "Alcoholism."

"And it has boxes for the patient—our sainted birth mother—spouse, parents, grandparents. That should make for an interesting inventory."

"Got the guts to ask?" I thought she did, probably more than I did.

"Hey, if she's willing to let me start with the form, I'm just going down the list and checking the boxes. She can react however she wants. I'll just feel lucky if we even get that far."

* * *

I had brought a small tape recorder, the kind lawyers used before dictation went out of style. If Sarah proved to be in a receptive mood, I didn't want to rely on my memory of her life story. That's what I wanted. Her life story, from beginning to end, with a special stop in the middle for the big question: Why?

Tibby and I sat on a low sofa across from Sarah, who had settled into what was obviously her favorite spot, a reclining wing chair incongruously constructed out of rattan—Chippendale meets Malaysia. Linda sat in a high-backed chair to Sarah's left. I nodded to Tibby and she dug into her bottomless purse for my tape recorder. I took it from her as casually as possible and placed it, along with a stack of tiny blank tapes, on the coffee table in front of us. The tapes clattered on the table's glass top.

Sarah had been talking to Linda, but now directed her gaze at the tape recorder. "What's that?"

"Just a little tape recorder," I answered innocently. "I thought you wouldn't mind." Liar.

"What do you need that for?" Sarah's tone was just short of shrill.

"I want to remember this day." Syrupy seemed like a good approach. "I want to hear stories about your childhood and your parents. And I don't want to lose the details." I looked into her eyes with as sincere an expression as I could muster. "This day is important to me."

"And you know I want to get your medical history," Linda chimed in. I had hoped we could raise that subject a little later, after our birth mother had gotten comfortable with us. Sarah turned her gaze slowly toward Linda, looking as if she was under assault.

"I promise you that no one other than the three of us will ever hear these tapes." That was a promise I could keep. "No big deal." I hoped that I hadn't irrevocably affected the tone of the conversation I wanted to have.

Sarah sat silently, deciding what to do. She wanted our attention, but on what terms? I debated whether to toss the recorder into Tibby's bag and end the standoff. It didn't seem fair trying to force my will on my birth mother, but I decided to forge ahead.

I pretended that the controversy was over. "I'd love to start at the beginning, where you were born and on from there. You were born in Lexington, right?"

Sarah looked at me, then at Linda, and back to me. "Yes, that's right. But we lived in a little town a few miles out."

"What was that like?" Linda asked. "A nice place to grow up?"

"Oh, yes." Sarah was warming to the subject, the tape recorder forgiven for the moment. "Not much there, a general store and station for the Norfolk & Western where you could flag down the train to New York."

"Wasn't your father a big shot with the railroad?" Linda had heard a lot of the story before and knew some of the topics that our birth mother would enjoy.

Sarah nodded. "He supervised the whole system in the area. And his father had run the general store." She laughed. "We seemed like the rich people in town, but that wasn't saying much."

Linda reached down to the side of her chair, pulled some papers from her bag, and picked up a magazine from a pile on the coffee table. "Since we're talking about your father and grandfather, maybe this is a good time to ask about their health."

She held the magazine as a writing platform under the medical-history form. Clicking a ballpoint pen in her right hand as she spoke: "You know I want to get everybody's medical history for my kids. I guess we've talked about that over the years, but now I want to do it right. I have this standard form, so I thought we could just go down it while we talked."

I couldn't decide whether the health quiz would be a useful

diversion or an annoying interruption. I knew the approach I wanted
to take with Sarah, but Linda had as much right to control the process
as I did. If I had my way, I would take Sarah's deposition the way I had
been taught to do it as a young lawyer.

* * *

Depositions are the formal process through which a lawyer interviews his adversary's witnesses before trial, with a court reporter taking
down every word. There are many books on the art of taking depositions, but my approach had always been to question the witness in
a methodical, almost rhythmic, process that relentlessly followed the
chronology of the events in question. I also liked to circle back briefly
to points I had covered earlier, asking slightly different questions to see
if I got consistent answers. My techniques weren't unique or particularly sophisticated, but they had worked for me in the past. I wanted to
rely on them in taking my most important deposition.

Sarah finally seemed to have forgotten the tape recorder, paying it
no attention even when I leaned forward to change the tape every half
hour. She was enjoying the opportunity to talk about herself before a
new audience. My birth mother had a highly mobile face; it twisted and
turned to match her emotions. She frequently brought her left hand
up across that side of her face, covering an eye and her forehead. Her
fingers were long and bony, seemingly gnarled by arthritis, although
she never mentioned suffering from the ailment that had destroyed
my knees.

We arrived at her relationship with her much older sister Charlotte.
I knew only that they'd been estranged for many years, and I didn't
think that Linda or Ellie knew much more. "And you haven't had any
contact with her for how long?" Linda was leading the charge.

"Since the 1960s, I guess. I'm an old woman. It's hard for me to
remember when things happened." I thought she had shown quick

recall of most events so far.

Linda pressed on. "Because of Maude? The accident?" I had heard enough about this from Ellie and Greg that I had made the story part of my fiction writing. I wanted to see how close I had come.

"No. Yes." Sarah seemed not to have decided. "I guess indirectly. I had had enough of her whining." Her head bobbed up and down as she spoke, emphasizing each word. "Always feeling sorry for herself."

I wanted to start at the beginning of the story, not the end. "Tell me about the accident. When was this?"

"I was still just a baby, four years old. Charlotte was seventeen and Maude was eight."

Sarah seemed willing enough to talk about the events, but my sister was anxious. "And Charlotte took you and Maude out in the car when she wasn't supposed to?" Stop leading the witness, Linda, I thought to myself.

The old lady nodded. "Some of her friends had come out from Lexington to go swimming. Father had told her, 'Don't you go and take them back into town. You're all going to be tired and I don't want you driving.' But Charlotte did it anyway. That's the way she was." Sarah had been twisting a handkerchief in her hands all afternoon, dabbing occasionally at a runny nose. She paused to dig the handkerchief from between her leg and the chair cushion. "The bootlegger's wife was drunk, Father was sure of it. She hit us broadside at a crossroad."

"Maude died on the scene?" Linda seemed to be following a script that she knew well.

Sarah nodded again, slowly. "I injured my leg. Nobody else was hurt. Except Charlotte was never the same."

"How did she handle it?"

"Badly, of course. She ran away a couple times. I think she was depressed from then on. You don't recover from something like that. I know our family was never the same." Sarah seemed detached from what must have been the singular event of her childhood, even if it was seventy-five years in the past.

"So what happened in the 1960s between you and Charlotte?" It was my turn to lead the witness.

"She was visiting us from Richmond for a few weeks. She always seemed to want to hang around here, always under foot."

"Here, in this house?"

"No, the one up the street where we lived way back when, where the kids grew up. I was working in the kitchen when Charlotte started whining about her life. She didn't say it, but I knew she meant the accident and killing Maude. I just had enough, so I told her to get out of the house. I sent her back to Richmond."

Sarah's voice had picked up the anger she felt at the time. "Never spoke to her again." She brought both hands up to her face, forming a mask with her fingers. She didn't seem particularly upset to me. I wondered whether the gesture was just a performance for our sake.

"Did Charlotte try to get in touch with you?" I suspected that Linda was asking another question for which she already had the answer.

"Oh, yes. She called all the time." Sarah spoke energetically, without a hint of embarrassment. "I always made Dan answer calls anyway, and I would just shake my head and refuse to come to the phone." Sarah's eyes moved over each of our faces. "That's awful, I know. I just had enough of her."

We were silent. She was right; it *was* awful. And it felt like the kind of truth I wanted to get from my birth mother.

Sarah filled the gap quietly. "She's probably dead now. She was born in 1910."

* * *

"Where were we? Oh, yeah. High blood pressure. Did either of Dan's parents have high blood pressure?" Linda had picked up the medical-history forms again. We didn't seem to be getting much useful information from the exercise. I stood up to stretch; we had been sitting in Sarah's sun room for nearly two hours and she wasn't showing any signs of flagging.

"I guess that's it for Dan and his side. Let's finish you." Linda pointed her pen to the top of the form.

Sarah sat back in her chair, smiling. She threw her arms in the air, laughed, and said, "I'm here to be finished off."

Linda moved quickly down the list, with Sarah answering 'no' to everything but allergies and migraines. Those symptoms generated an enthusiastic dialogue between the two women. I looked at my watch and at the darkening sky outside the windows. As soon as Linda got through "alcoholism" on the list, I was going to interrupt and chase after my own interests. Then it dawned on me that Linda was reciting ailments that were farther down the list than alcoholism. I smiled; my sister had decided to censor the list for Sarah's benefit. It seemed like a fine decision to me.

* * *

"Depression?" It was an important question, and thankfully the last on Linda's list.

Sarah's answer was quick and confident: "Wouldn't you be if you gave up a baby?"

Linda sympathized. "It must have been horrible. When you were first pregnant—with Greg—was that intended?"

"We didn't care. We just loved each other."

This was where I had been waiting to go. I spoke softly: "I know this is difficult for you, but I would like to talk about that time in your life. By my count, you were pregnant again within six months of Greg's birth. Was that a surprise?"

"Yeah, we were trying not to, but you don't always do the right thing."

"You mean trying to avoid getting pregnant?"

"Yes. We tried all kinds of methods. You were the diaphragm baby."

"Oh." I laughed self-consciously.

"We really messed up on that one. That nurse was an inexperienced fitter."

"I guess I'm not too sorry about that." It was good to be here.

Sarah and Linda laughed. My birth mother said, "I guess it's not nice to joke."

"About my almost non-existence?" I hoped that my lack of a sense of humor wasn't showing. "All I know is that the sperm that made me must have been a real fighter." Excellent deflection, I thought to myself.

26

Time was running short. We were supposed to meet Ellie for dinner, and I was ready to leave my birth mother behind for a while. It was clear that we would have more opportunities to see Sarah if we wanted them, so it no longer felt like a last-chance encounter. But I still had a few questions to ask.

"When you learned that you were pregnant for the second time...."

"I was glad." She interrupted with force, as if challenging an unstated assumption in my question.

"You were?"

"I thought, Oh, boy, we can have sex again!"

I blushed. It wasn't the answer that I expected. Linda chimed in. "I know what you mean, no diaphragm, no nothing."

Sarah looked at me and reacted to the puzzled look on my face: "I'm sorry. I just loved babies."

I tried to get back on track. "Okay. So what happened to cause you to give up the second baby?" Our oldest sister, Dawn.

Sarah's smile disappeared, a pout replacing it, her eyes downcast. "Things were getting pretty bad. Dan's father had lost his job and we had to help. It seemed like more money was going out of the house than coming in."

"Was it a joint decision to give up the baby?" I thought there had to be a single villain in the story. My vote was for Dan Jones, of course.

"Yes it was. We sat down and discussed it. These were pretty glum times, awful times for us." We were all silent. I hoped that neither

Linda nor Tibby would feel compelled to step in for Sarah. I wanted to hear more, without influencing the flow.

She obliged. "We seemed to be getting it coming and going. Do we give a young baby that didn't know us a chance and just let the older people go? They were people who had taken care of us." She seemed to anticipate the next question, although it wouldn't have been my next question. "Then, by the time Mary came along, our economics had improved."

Your economics had improved? I thought to myself. That sounded like a company's earnings report for the third quarter. How many times had she practiced that line in her mind? I began to see less importance in the questions I asked.

"Ever consider abortion?" Hey, if the diaphragm couldn't stop me, how about a trip to the bad side of town, or wherever abortions were performed in those days?

"Oh, no. We would never have done that."

"For religious reasons?" I had never heard that religion was a part of their lives.

Sarah spoke firmly. "No. I told you: We just loved babies."

Linda offered sympathy. "It must have been torture to be pregnant for all those years."

Sarah put on a sad-doll face, eyes again studying the floor. "It was," she said softly.

I was struggling. "You had to be pregnant for most of, what, seven years with kids you weren't going to keep. Nobody ever knew?"

"I was very thin. I hid it very well."

Linda nodded. "No one knew I was pregnant with Matt at eight months. I didn't want anyone to know. It was none of their business."

Sarah shuddered. "Everyone patting your belly."

"Exactly." Linda wasn't placating her birth mother. They seemed to be in synch, at least on this small point. I felt like I was watching from the sidelines. Sarah would have hidden even the Keeper pregnancies from the neighbors' eyes, and Linda understood.

Sarah wasn't finished: "One of the nosy neighbors guessed I was pregnant with one of you. Later I told her," here Sarah mimicked her mourning performance, "'That baby just didn't make it.'" She laughed sourly.

∗ ∗ ∗

Where was my birth father in all of this? Just an accountant going over the family's weak finances, laying babies off the payroll? I wouldn't be able to assess him with my own eyes, but I hoped that Sarah could show me something more.

"How did your husband handle all of this at the time?" I was still fumbling with what to call Dan Jones.

"He was sad, but it was what had to be done. He just put it out of his mind afterward. That was the way he was. The girls would probably say he was staid. He just didn't show a lot of emotion about anything."

"So the two of you never talked about giving away a baby once it was done?"

"That's right. We just went on." It was what it was.

"That didn't make it more difficult for you as a mother giving up children, not having anyone to talk with about...."

Sarah cut me off with a wave of her hand. "I saw Dan's point: There wasn't anything to talk about." It seemed to me that there would have been a lot to talk about.

"David asked me how much Dan knew about us being in contact with you." Linda had put away the medical-history forms and seemed to appreciate that this was the time to grab what we could from Sarah. "I'm pretty sure he listened in on some of my phone calls with you."

Sarah seemed hesitant. "I don't know about that. Listened into calls? Well, maybe. I don't know."

"I remember that time you threw me in front of Dan when I was visiting you and he came out of his room. I'm still mad at you about that." Linda laughed to show that she wasn't that mad. "He must have known what was going on then. Did he say anything to you about it?"

"Not a word."

"But what about when David, Tibby, and I visited you at the hotel? I know you told him then where you were going when you walked down the street with Ellie to meet us."

"He just said, 'Fine. Do what you think best.'"

Linda had taken over as inquisitor. "What did he say when you came back?"

"He asked if we had a good meeting. Nothing else. I said 'yes' and that was the end of it."

I sat back, listening to the conversation between my birth mother and her third daughter. They had a twenty-year relationship. Linda had heard so much of this over the years, but I still found it hard to digest.

I wanted to add color to the picture, floundering for insights into a man I was finding deficient. "Did he have a good sense of humor?"

Sarah didn't seem surprised by the question. "Oh, yes. He was a quiet man, but he could be very outgoing, depending on where he was. Like I said, the kids thought he was staid, stuffy." That might have been the way people described me, too. "Greg said he wanted to kill Dan, said he was spanked, beaten all the time. I saw it only once. Of course," she lowered her voice conspiratorially, "I think Greg's nuts."

"So Dan didn't get angry much?" I didn't want the discussion to shift to Greg.

"No. You never really saw anger out of him."

Linda wasn't ready to let that pass. "I thought you told me there were times when Dan was out of control, drinking too much. Wasn't there the time that he fell into the coffee table, he was so drunk? Remember? You took the kids out of the house and spent the night in the car, right?"

Sarah looked embarrassed, upset that her confidences were being exposed. "He…I…I don't remember that. He was never abusive to the kids, I'm sure. He might drink too much. He was a very mild man, even drunk."

She shifted in her seat and jabbed her finger in the direction of my tape recorder. Raising her voice and looking angrily at me: "Are you taping that?"

Startled, I stammered, "Yes, ma'am."

Sarah spoke sharply. "Why?"

"Like I said before, I want to remember…."

"You don't want to remember your father like that," she snapped.

How could I remember a man I never knew? I didn't ask Sarah that question.

∗ ∗ ∗

Sarah led us slowly toward the door, seeming reluctant to let us leave. Linda spoke up in a sing-song tone: "Why don't you give us a tour on the way out? I'm sure Tibby and David would like to see where you and Dan lived for all these years."

Sarah looked uneasy, but seemed to decide that a tour would at least be a way to keep us there a while longer. "Oh, all right, I suppose. But there isn't much to see…."

Linda cut her off. "Let's start in there." She pointed to the room that I had guessed was the master bedroom when we first came into the house. As Sarah turned to the doorway, Linda looked at me, raised her eyebrows twice, and tipped her head in that direction, nodding quickly as if to say, "Check this out."

The room seemed ordinary enough, centered by a double bed with a white chenille bedspread like the ones my grandmother had favored thirty years before. Standard pieces of bedroom furniture ran along the walls. Curtains were pulled partway across the room's two windows, the light rendered dimmer by the early winter dusk.

Linda pulled me toward the large, white-wicker baby crib I had spotted from the entry hall when we first came into the house. She squeezed my arm, signaling an unspoken conversation between the two of us, as she cooed at the old woman. "Oh, look at the baby doll. That's so cute, Sarah." A full-sized doll stared out from under the elaborate covers of the crib, its face framed by a lacy bonnet. It appeared life-like, more natural than a store mannequin, with the flesh tones of a newborn. I stared at the doll, captivated by the eeriness of the crib and its contents at the foot of the old woman's bed, then turned quickly away before Sarah could see any reaction on my face.

"Mary gave her to me. She knows how much I love babies." Sarah had moved to the side of the crib, looking lovingly down at the thing. "I *do* love babies. Isn't it perfect?"

I walked toward the doorway, intent on getting on with the tour. I wanted to leave behind the creepy shrine to all the babies my birth mother had given up. I was the failed-diaphragm baby, the accidental child of a woman who said she loved babies. I was glad not to have ever been the baby in the crib at the foot of Sarah Jones's bed.

∗ ∗ ∗

"You mean it was all a wonderful life?" Ellie looked as if she had been slapped as she spat out the words. Tibby, Linda, and I had met her at a stylish restaurant in the center of town. An open kitchen, an interesting wine list, a menu whose descriptions had a high adjective-to-noun ratio. Just the kind of place I liked, a perfect place to recover from the day.

Linda sat next to Ellie, across the softly lit table from Tibby and me. Linda turned to her sister. "Yeah. Can you believe it?" Her tone became sarcastic. "They were completely happy together, just couldn't keep the babies they loved because of money problems." Linda sounded offended on her sister's behalf.

"They must have lived in a different house than the one I grew up in." Ellie began to ask Linda a string of "what about" questions. What about this or that damaging event in Ellie's childhood? I listened quietly to the dialogue, totally sympathetic to how my youngest sister must have felt when her suffering was reduced to no consequence.

I studied Ellie's face, her words disappearing into the background. She had lived in that house, had grown up with the father who would always be unknown to me, but she didn't have any more of the answers than I did.

I had all the answers I was going to get from Sarah. She loved babies, even kept a surrogate at the foot of her bed, but had given away four of her own. She loved babies, but hid all of her pregnancies from the neighbors. She loved babies, but never seemed interested in learning what happened to me. Sarah saw her husband and herself as stoics, silent in the aftermath of impossible decisions, but the Keepers' home was not a peaceful one. She thought that hers had been a happy marriage; I believed her and, at the same time, was sure that she was wrong. She was still writing her story, just as I had, but no longer knew which parts were truth and which were fiction.

I had gone deep into the turtle hole. I had asked as many questions as I could and would have to be satisfied with the answers I got.

* * *

My need for completeness, my drive for all of the truth and a believable story, had pushed me to write fiction. I had thought that it was a harmless exercise in filling the gaps. Now there were fewer gaps as I sat there listening to my sisters, but the picture wasn't going to be much easier to recognize than when I had resorted to fiction to sharpen it. I understood that the Throwaways, and the Keepers for that matter, were the result of my parents' dysfunction, not the cause of it. I just didn't know what *was* the cause. And now I saw that I never would.

It would have been a difficult conversation to have had ten years before with the thirty-nine-year-old me, the guy who was just about to start the serious search for his older brother. He would have rejected the concept of being satisfied with anything other than the whole truth, of starting on a trip that might end anywhere other than the destination he perceived as ideal. That guy would have believed there was only complete success or utter failure at the end of the line. That's why taking risks would have been so dangerous for the younger me, with failure the only alternative to perfection. But that me had a lot to learn about humanity, about impossible standards imposed on imperfect lives.

By the time I was sitting in that restaurant, listening to my sisters, and thinking about Sarah's love for babies, I was finally beginning to see the alternative endings, even the happy endings, that might present themselves if I only knew to look for them.

27

Tibby and I had decided to move from our house in suburban Bethesda to a century-old condominium building in one of Washington's historic districts. We loved the twenty-three years we had spent in the house, but wanted a change. We traveled a lot and usually found ourselves wandering the busy streets of interesting cities. We were city people at heart, so why not live that way?

We spent six months renovating a fifth-floor apartment that had been lived in for sixty years by a cranky widow, a haughty dowager empress, judging from the stories we heard. She had died a few years before, leaving her heirs an apartment that hadn't seen improvement since the 1970s. We liked the idea of starting with a clean slate, not having to pay for someone else's taste only to tear out their mistakes before making our own.

I worked at home by now, a side benefit of leaving the full-time practice of law. So it had been important for me to carve out a little office from a warren of dark closets that were empty but for somebody's dead houseplant the day we first saw the place.

I was sitting at my computer one afternoon when Ellie called. I'd been hunched over the keyboard tapping out aggravated emails on my latest deal and welcomed the break in concentration when I saw her number pop up on caller ID.

"Hey, Tallmouse!" That was Ellie's email alias. "What's up?"

"Got a few minutes?" She never called from the office during a work day. I should have taken the hint, but didn't.

"I dunno. You're dragging me away from the equivalent of a knife fight by email, so it had better be good. Actually, thanks for the call. My blood pressure's dropping already."

"I hope I don't raise it." No humor in her voice.

"Everything okay?"

"Not really. I'm a little embarrassed to have waited so long to tell you the news about Mom. I…I just have so many conflicts to process. Anyway, Mom's in a nursing home." I sagged in my chair; nursing homes were usually the end of the line.

"Man, I'm really sorry, Ellie. What happened?"

"She got taken to the emergency room a little over a week ago. A fall after she got her hands on alcohol again."

Ellie's voice sharpened. "I have my suspicions where she got it from, and it makes me so angry. But that's for later."

She paused, knowing the effect her next words would have. "The doctors say her liver's gone. Maybe one to four months left."

I said nothing for a moment, unsure of my own thoughts. Then, "What can I do to help?" I was already feeling guilty. I spoke to Sarah a couple of times a year, always promising to go down for a visit. She seemed genuinely pleased whenever I made the suggestion, but I was sure that she agonized over the idea of seeing me again.

A day after my last phone call to Sarah, Greg's new wife, Tina, had called, an unusual event. Our relationship was pleasant enough, but we didn't really know each other. I had a stronger relationship with Hannah, Tina's predecessor, a sore point with Greg.

Tina got to the point quickly: "I wanted to let you know that Sarah called here a little while ago. She was very upset and asked me to call you and apologize, but she just couldn't handle meeting your mother. She says you want to take your mother to meet her, and it's got her panicked. "

"Tina, I have no idea what she's talking about. I called her to wish her a happy birthday. We had a nice conversation." It had barely been five minutes long; Sarah and I didn't really know what to say to each other. "But I didn't mention my mom at all, and certainly didn't say anything about putting the two of them together." I had tried that idea out on Sarah just once, soon after our first meeting. She saw it only as an opportunity for shame and humiliation, no matter how much I told her about my mother's desire to thank her for letting me be part of my parents' lives.

"Yeah, I guessed as much," she said knowingly. "Sarah's mind seems to be going. One minute sharp as ever, the next remembering things that might not have happened. Don't worry about it. I'll call her and calm her down." I was grateful for the offer, as I didn't want to call Sarah myself, starting the cycle again.

* * *

Ellie's voice had flattened. "There isn't a thing you can do. I don't think there's anything anyone can do. But you should also know that Mary is trying to make *sure* there's nothing you or Linda or Noelle can do." Ellie and her sister had been at odds about Sarah. Ellie had tried to limit her own exposure to her mother, while still helping Mary manage the details of an old woman's life.

"How's that?" I hadn't given much thought to Mary for a long time. My sense was that she felt martyred by her lead role in her mother's life.

"She went into the nursing home waving her power of attorney around. No one's allowed to visit Mom without Mary's permission."

"Even you?"

Ellie drew in her breath. "No, I guess I'm on the approved list. It's just that…. It's hard to admit, but I still haven't been to see her. I will, but I'm struggling with it right now."

I was surprised that Sarah's condition hadn't broken Ellie's resistance to seeing her mother, but it showed that I was still underestimating the traumas of Ellie's childhood. My surprise was only that; I wasn't prepared to judge her for her reluctance.

"Have you told Linda and Noelle?" Ellie wouldn't have thought to call our sister Dawn, who had kept her distance from Sarah even after the old woman had expressed a willingness to meet. I had fought hard to engineer their reunion—so long after Sarah's abusive response to the first Throwaways' appearance on her doorstep. In hindsight, getting the two of them together would have spurred me to a final visit with Sarah before it had become too late.

"I just talked to Noelle, but not Linda yet. Maybe you could call her first? I'm exhausted."

"Sure. You know she's going to want to go down there to see Sarah. They've been through a lot together, and for a long time."

Ellie sighed. "I know she'll want to. But we need to convince her it's not a good idea. I think Mary is dead serious about keeping y'all away from Mom. It's sad, but it would get ugly if you tried to do anything about it. I'm sorry. Nice family, huh?"

* * *

I had drifted out of my office into the living room, dropping into one of the big upholstered chairs that let me look up through our windows at the ornate apartment building across Connecticut Avenue. I loved the gargoyles that were spaced along the edge of the building's roof: Ten bare-chested, horned devils holding spherical boulders over their heads, nasty grins on their faces as they waited to pelt unsuspecting pedestrians on the sidewalk below.

I tried to get away from my computer screen, and its temptations, when I wanted to focus on the person on the other end of the line. As I listened to Ellie, I looked out through the old, wavy glass in our windows. Rocking my head from side to side caused the distortions in the window glass to make the stone gargoyles move. They were coming alive, finally free to throw the rocks they'd held frozen over their heads for so long.

Sometimes, looking down through that wavy glass at the traffic moving by our building, I wanted to rub my eyes, as if that could sharpen the wobbly images. Sarah's decline drew me back to her distorted memories of a happy family life. She wouldn't have rubbed her eyes to sharpen her memory. Her old glass let her see things just the way she needed to see them.

* * *

Tibby's keys rattled in the lock. She pushed the front door open, hands filled with her two purses and a bag of groceries. I jumped up from my desk and, after untangling the straps and bag handles from her arms, followed her into the kitchen juggling the groceries and one of her big purses. It astonished me that she could hoof around every day with so much heavy stuff on her arms. Then again I was always happy to throw my sunglasses or camera into one of her bags when we headed out the door together.

Tibby walked in and out of the pantry closet as I talked through my conversation with Ellie, then the harder call I'd had to make to Linda. I leaned against the kitchen counter, lowering and raising my voice as she came and went. "Still feeling sympathetic toward Mary? Linda was pretty upset, like you'd expect. She seemed ready to drop everything and go see Sarah. It's infuriating that anyone would tell Linda she can't spend time with a dying old lady."

"How did she handle the news about Mary's roadblock?" Tibby stopped putting away the groceries and turned toward me.

"Like she should have. First, she said she didn't care what Mary wanted. She and Noelle had been closer to Sarah—better friends— than any of her family had been for a long time. That kind of thing. And I think she's probably right. So we started to joke around about how we'd dress up like orderlies with bedpans or something and sneak in. You know the way we talk, especially when we're trying to act like we're not as upset as we really are."

"Yeah. I know." Tibby wasn't a fan of our sarcastic humor.

"Hey, Linda's worked up. She cares about Sarah; I guess I do, too, at a different level. She feels helpless, and I can't see what Mary gets out of inflicting needless pain. It sounds like Sarah might not be alert enough to know Linda's there, but I bet she'd be happy to see her if she could. And Mary apparently found a lot of old letters from Linda in Sarah's house, so she knows that they have a long history together—one that Sarah obviously encouraged. So what's in it for her? Just plain vindictiveness?"

Tibby shook her head. "That's too easy. She's a troubled woman from a troubled family. She might not be able to admit it, but look at her sister. Ellie gets that she was injured by her upbringing. Some people can face it; others can't. It's hard to do right now, but Mary deserves pity more than anger. Maybe someday she'll have to deal with the fact that she hurt Linda and Noelle. And what about you?"

"Me?"

"You. How do you feel about being shut out from seeing Sarah?"

"To be honest, I'm not sure I would have wanted to go down and see her in the nursing home. We've already been in too many of those with my dad and your mother. I don't think she would have gotten much out of it, and I know I wouldn't have. Now...."

I had stopped for the first time since hanging up with Ellie to consider how I felt. "Her funeral is a different story. The idea of not being there feels very wrong."

Tibby was right. I didn't need to be angry at my sister Mary. Something ugly made it impossible for her to see what she was missing by excluding the Throwaways from her life. It made me think of the dancing gargoyles, and I laughed as I said so out loud.

"The what?" She was used to my foolishness.

"The dancing gargoyles. I was looking at them this afternoon. Come here." She followed me into the living room. "See? Stand here and look up at the gargoyles. Now move your head from side to side. They're alive!" I was a kid showing off his latest discovery.

Tibby didn't seem that moved by the experience. "Great. What's that got to do with Mary?"

"Aw, come on. You don't like my masterful, literary metaphor? It's the wavy glass. We all see life through wavy glass. Mary's is just wavier than some. She sees things differently than we do. Get it?" I was really warming to my insight. "And Sarah, too. If I'm okay with Sarah seeing things the way they weren't, I guess I have to let Mary off the hook."

Tibby gave me her thoughtful look, the one that said I was trying too hard to make a simple point.

*　*　*

"Thought you'd want to see this." I handed the single sheet of paper to Tibby, a printout of a Web page. "'The services will be private.'" I laughed without humor. "Just like Dan Jones's funeral, courtesy of Mary, I guess."

Tibby scanned the details of Sarah's obituary. The doctor's one-to-four-month prognosis had been optimistic. Sarah died only a few weeks later in the nursing home, spending those last days slipping in and out of limited consciousness. I hadn't pressed Ellie for details, so it was a vague experience for me. Tibby handed the page back without comment. She watched me to see where I was heading.

"Even though I saw the same thing in Dan Jones's obituary, it's still kind of entertaining to see the recital of the children she's survived by. Too bad this isn't like a Wikipedia entry, so that I could go in and edit that part to include the Throwaways."

"Would you want to do that?" She knew the answer.

I shook my head. "But there is an online guest book for comments. How about a few words of condolence there from her second son? Or a bouquet with three white roses and four black ones with a card saying 'From the Keepers and the Throwaways?'"

"Two excellent ideas. But seriously, now that you've had time to think about it, would you go to the funeral if…."

"If Mary wasn't guarding the door to the church with a shotgun?" I smiled.

Tibby didn't return the smile. "Mary's not the issue here, at least not the only one. What about Sarah herself?"

I had learned as a lawyer that defining the real issue—not what the client might think is the issue—is the key to the legal analysis. Even with that hard-won perspective, I had often managed to miss the point in my own life. I would chase so blindly after my goal of the moment that I didn't see the unexpected opportunities. I only wanted to find my mythically defined brother, so my Throwaway sisters had to find me. I sought perfect knowledge of my birth parents' motives, wasting time on fiction to fill the void, rather than studying the clues around me. Clues that would have made more obvious what my birth mother had to show me through her faded memory.

Sarah Jones loved babies, not the people they would become. An inanimate object in a crib at the foot of her bed memorialized the center of her devotion.

I spoke quietly. "Sarah wouldn't have wanted us there, either. She spent her life making sure it wouldn't happen." A sad conclusion, yet I felt redeemed, not rejected. Our birth mother couldn't give us what she didn't have. It was, in the end, nothing personal.

My wife stared at me, puzzled by the smile on my face. "What?" she asked, as if missing the joke.

I laughed. "I can stop trying to write fiction now, can't I?"

ABOUT THE AUTHOR

When he isn't writing, or pursuing his enthusiasm for photography, David Ford works with businesses ranging from start-ups to industry leaders. For the first two decades of his professional career, he was an attorney in private practice in Washington, D.C. His business life is now largely dedicated to seniors housing and issues relating to elder care.

His published writings range from a political-humor piece in the Washington Post to technical articles in mind-numbing legal journals. Visit *www.blindinoneeye.com* to contact him.